Concept of Truth in Science and Religion

About the Authors

Prof. K.D. Gangrade (*b.* 1926), Vice-Chairman of Gandhi Smriti and Darshan Samiti, New Delhi, has been a former Pro-Vice-Chancellor, Dean Faculty of Social Sciences, and Head, Department of Social Work University of Delhi. He has also taught at the University of Mancheste U.K. and Tata Institute of Social Sciences, Mumbai. He has served th United Nations as well in various capacities. Prof. Gangrade has 12 book to his credit. He is recipient of Samaj Gaurav (1988) from the Bhartiy Sangthan, Rashtra Ratna (1998) from Viswa Jagriti Mission, and Radh Raman Award (2000) for outstanding contribution to education.

Dr. Laxman Singh Kothari (*b.* 1926) obtained his M.Sc. (Physics) degre from University of Delhi and Ph.D. degree from Bombay University. O Atomic Energy Establishment scholarship he spent about 4 years a Cambridge, Oxford and Saclay (France) working on problems connecte with atomic energy (1951-54). He joined the Establishment (now Bhabh Atomic Research Establishment) and served there in various capacities including Head of the Theoretical Physics Group (1954-61). He joined Delh University as Reader in Physics (1962-63) and was elevated to th prestigious chair of Sir Shri Ram Professor (1963-91).

He has done outstanding work on interaction of thermal neutron wit solids and published over 170 research papers in national and internationa journals. He has edited 4 books and written two more on technical subjects He has also written 3 books in English and 2 in Hindi for school children He is a Fellow of the Indian National Science Academy and served as Editor of Publications (1975-78) and Treasurer (1989-92).

Dr. Ajit Ram Verma (*b.* 1921) took his M.Sc. (Physics) degree fror Allahabad University and obtained his Ph.D. and D.Sc. degrees fror University of London, U.K. He was also awarded D.Sc. (Honoris Causa) by Banaras Hindu University in 2000.

He served as Reader in Physics at Delhi University (1955-59) and as Professor and Head of the Physics Department at Banaras Hind University (1959-65). He was the Director of the National Physica Laboratory (1965-82). He was Visiting Professor at IIT Delhi for three year (1982-85).

He has done outstanding research work on crystal growth which i internationally recognized. While at NPL he introduced quantur standards. He has written four technical books and published over 8 research papers in national and international journals. Also he has to hi credit four books, one in English and three in Hindi on popular scienc subjects. Dr. Verma was awarded Atma Ram Award by the Kendriya Hind Sansthan, Agra for his contributions. He has also received Shanti Swaru Bhatnagar Award for his research in Physics. Dr. Verma was awarde Padma Bhushan by President of India in 1982 for his outstandin contribution to science.

CONCEPT OF TRUTH IN SCIENCE AND RELIGION

K.D. GANGRADE
L.S. KOTHARI
A.R. VERMA

Gandhi Smriti and Darshan Samiti,
Rajghat, New Delhi
and
Professor D.S. Kothari Centre for
Science, Ethics and Education
University of Delhi, Delhi
by
CONCEPT PUBLISHING COMPANY, NEW DELHI-110059

Cataloging in Publication Data—DK
Courtesy: D.K. Agencies (P) Ltd. <docinfo@dkagencies.com>

Gangrade, K. D. (Kesharichand Dasharathasa), 1926-
Concept of truth in science and religion / K.D. Gangrade, L.S. Kothari, A.R. Verma.
p. cm.
Includes bibliographical references.
Includes index.
ISBN 818069190X

1. Philosophy and science. 2. Religion and science. 3. Philosophy, Indic. I. Kothari, L. S. (Laxman Singh), 1926- joint author. II. Verma, A. R. (Ajit Ram), 1921- joint author. III. Title.

DDC 291.175 21

ISBN: 81-8069-190-X

First Published 2005

Published and Printed by
Ashok Kumar Mittal
Concept Publishing Company,
A/15-16, Commercial Block, Mohan Garden,
New Delhi-110059 (INDIA)

Phones : 25351460, 25351794
Fax : 091-11-25357103
Email : publishing@conceptpub.com

Preface

Recently Professor D.S. Kothari Centre for Science, Ethics and Education, of the University of Delhi brought out three books. The first one — *Education and Character Building*, is a collection of Convocation Addresses delivered by the late Professor D.S. Kothari at various Universities in India between 1962 to 1983 and was published in 2000. Various Memorial Lectures, delivered by him during 1959 to 1987 were collected and published in 2002 under the title *Atom and Self*. His lectures on University Education and Defence Science have recently been brought out under the title *Knowledge and Wisdom* (2003).

The Memorial Lectures were delivered at various institutions including National Physical Laboratory, Sir Shriram Institute of Industrial Research, and Indian National Science Academy. Some of the lectures were organised by Societies/ Trusts formed in the memory of great men. These included Professor Meghnad Saha Memorial Lecture, Sir Shanti Swarup Bhatnagar Memorial Lecture, Azad Memorial Lecture and Dada Bhai Naoroji Memorial Lecture. Apart from a few lectures, which were on technical subjects, Professor Kothari mainly talked about the close relationship between science and ethics, and science and ancient Indian philosophy. These lectures were addressed to university scholars and Fellows of Academies.

We had the privilege of coming in close contact with the late Professor Kothari (1906-1993) on many occasions and had in-depth discussions on wide ranging subjects. He was not only an outstanding physicist but also a deep thinker. In dedicating his book '*Meaning and Medicine*' (Bantam Books, 1991), Dr. Larry Dossey wrote: "Dr. Kothari spoke the languages of modern physics and the ancient Upanishads with equal profundity and grace. In his life and philosophy he has honoured the realities of the physical, mental, and spiritual as few scientists I have known". We feel that the thoughts presented by Professor Kothari are of great relevance to our needs of the day.

Professor Kothari was a great admirer of Gandhi and quoted him extensively in his lectures. He regarded Gandhi as a man with a true scientific spirit as is reflected by the fact that his autobiography is titled *'Story of My Experiments with Truth'*. We have here attempted to present his and other scientists' views on Science and Truth, as we understood them.

We would like to thank Professor Feroz Ahmed, Co-ordinator, Professor D.S. Kothari Centre for Science, Ethics and Education for his constant help and Mr. Achuta Nand Rai and Mr. Puran Singh Mandal for their help in preparing the manuscript.

Contents

Part I

1

Introduction

We are living in very turbulent times. On the one hand, man has landed on the moon and successfully exploited the energy stored inside nuclei of atoms. The advances made in communication technology are mind-boggling. Who could have imagined, even a few years ago that one would be able to instantaneously establish contacts with almost anyone around the world at nearly zero cost? Recent advances made in the medical field have totally changed our concept of health care.

Yet on the other hand we seem to be living in continuous tension with most of our neighbours. There are conflicts and quarrels among communities and threats of war still exist. The graph of crime is increasing day by day and citizens feel unsafe even at home. Man has perhaps become a misfit in the present setting.

We observe a rapidly growing gulf between the physical and cultural aspects of man. Culturally man evolves very gradually and it may take centuries before any noticeable changes are observed in man's nature and behaviour. On the other hand physical environment, which depends upon science and technology, changes very rapidly.

It has been observed that for the past few centuries scientific knowledge doubles in every ten years. We may consider the number of working scientists, or the number of research papers published, or the number of journals published, we will arrive at the same conclusion. This exponential growth of scientific knowledge makes a very significant impact on the life of man. For one thing, because of this, almost 90 per cent of the scientists that ever lived are alive today! The other more important result is that the gap between the developed and the underdeveloped (developing) countries goes on increasing rapidly.

Let us suppose that at a given point of time two countries — A and B are respectively at levels 1 and 5 of development, on a certain scale. The difference in their development, at the start is thus 4 points. After 10 years the two countries will be respectively at levels 2 and 10, with a difference in their development having increased to 8 points. After 50 years this difference would have increased to over 50 points. In a century this difference will be over 1,000 points. In India one can almost notice this galloping gap. Before independence our contribution to world science was a significant part of the whole, but as years passed by, the gap between the level of science being done here and outside has widened very significantly [as is also clear from recent studies reported in Current Science **83**, 107-108 (2002)].

Another important consequence of rapid advances in science is the shrinking time gap between a scientific invention and its practical use on a mass-scale. Whereas it took almost 100 years for the full practical use of photography after the discovery of its principle in 1727, it took only around 35 years for the development of radio broadcasting following the discovery of electromagnetic waves (1867). More recently we find that the time gap between the principle of solar cell (1953) and its practical use was reduced to two years. We can now feel the accelerating rate of advances taking place in information technology and the falling prices of new generation of computers. The great advantage of such rapid changes is mostly being exploited by the developed countries.

Man now faces two major problems: dehumanisation of man's relation with man and a deteriorating situation between man and nature. Machines have come to dominate every sphere of life, leading to greatly reduced human-human interaction. Man's desire to control and exploit nature has led to its grave degradation. We face river water pollution, environmental degradation, global warming, ozone depletion, leading to unforeseen and unpredictable climatic changes.

Where are we heading? Certainly not towards a peaceful,

harmonious world order. Some people feel that a way out of this difficulty is to put a stop to all further research in science and technology. They seem to forget that science has become so much an integral part of our life and culture that it would neither be desirable nor possible to do that. We do need science and more science. At the same time we must learn to use science for the good and betterment of humankind.

We observe the world around us mainly by sight and sound. We find that it is ever changing. Every individual forms a different opinion about what he observes. The perspectives can also be different—may be artistic, moral or religious. Yet we believe that there can be only one scientific truth with regard to nature, at least for us human beings, because there is only one humanity. Science looks for permanence in change.

Search for truths about nature is science. It is a creative activity. When one obtains a new insight into the working of nature, one is as much thrilled as say a painter or a sculptor when he creates a masterpiece. However, there is one major difference between science and the arts. Scientific effort is cumulative and co-operative, whereas each artistic creation is complete in itself. In science, every newly established fact, however insignificant it may appear to be at the time, and every new idea, however small, is bound sooner or later to contribute to major advances in our understanding of nature. Even such a great physicist as Newton wrote: "If I can see a little farther, it is by standing on the shoulders of giants."

Like religion, pursuit of science is one of the most selfless human activities. There are many branches of science, such as astronomy, cosmology, high energy particle physics, parts of geophysics, which are pursued with great devotion and in which enormous amount of money is spent, which have no possible applications as far as one can see. There have been people who have spent their entire life studying some very restricted aspect of nature, just watching birds for example or observing stars at night. This total commitment to a chosen field is not peculiar to men of science. We find this in saints and in all great artists, musicians, writers and others. One cannot define their motivation: in some sense it is service to God.

As Einstein put it, "The state of the mind that enables a man to do work of this kind is akin to that of the religious worshipper or the lover: the daily effort comes from no deliberate intentions or programme, but straight from the heart."

How science is used is not a part of science. What use we make of the discoveries of science is decided by man on considerations far removed from science. Man decides whether fire is to be used to cook food or burn houses; atomic energy is to be used to generate power or burst atomic bombs. Thus, apart from science, man needs ethics for progress. Religion provides a basis for ethics.

Science and religion both represent man's search for truth. There are roughly speaking three kinds of *truths*: (1) mathematical, (2) scientific, and (3) moral. In these are not included the fourth category of revealed or scriptural Truths. To a large measure these would fall under category (3). One can ask what is the nature of "proof", the criterion of validity, for the three kinds of truths? The important thing to notice is that the nature of proof is essentially different in the three cases.

Take the example of mathematical truth. The proof of a mathematical theorem consists in deducing it by pure reasoning, starting from some given axioms. It is an exercise in logical thought and nothing else. What is required of the axioms of a system is that these are not known to be mutually contradictory.

In the case of scientific truth the test consists in demonstrating that it explains (and predicts) results of experiments and observations. What is extremely important is to recognise that no observation, no measurement is possible without a proper theoretical framework. In science a theory or explanation is always tentative, waiting to be replaced by a more comprehensive theory. There is nothing like a 'true theory'. That represents an ideal—a limit that can never be attained. The notion of 'true theory' serves as a motivation for continuing improvement. Scientific truth is based on experience, while mathematical truth is based on pure logic. This distinction between mathematical truths and scientific truths is crucial.

Now we turn to *moral truths*. We all know that *ahimsa* is a good thing, but this cannot be proved by referring to books on mathematics or science, since both of these are neutral as regards morals. The concept of good or bad implies value judgements and values are related to purposes, aims and goals.

Bertrand Russel says in *Wisdom of the West* (1959):

> "We cannot give scientific justification for the goals that we might pursue, or for the ethical principles that we adopt.... No scientific reason can be given why it is bad to inflict wanton cruelty on one's fellows. To me it seems bad, and I image that this view is widely held. As to why cruelty is a bad thing, I am not sure that I can supply satisfactory reason."

Elsewhere Russel writes (*The Science to Save Us from Science*, 1950):

> "Science by itself, cannot supply us with an ethics. It can show us how to achieve a given end, and it may show us that some ends cannot be achieved. But among ends that can be achieved, our choice must be decided by other than purely scientific considerations."

What then is the test for a moral truth? Gandhiji said that for him the test of a moral principle was the willingness of the person who subscribed to it to suffer for it without harming the opponents. A moral principle is 'true' if it is in unison with man's spirit, if it is close to his 'soul'.

Science represents the external world and religion the internal world. Very often the two worlds are regarded as separate and totally disconnected. In this book we have attempted to show that there is no contradiction between science and religion. The unity and synthesis of the two streams of thoughts is what we want to emphasize.

For the progress of humanity we need both advancement of science as well as practice of ethics. This can be achieved only by providing sound education to all citizens. Particularly in developing countries, this is vitally important. The best investment a country can make is in providing sound education to all its children, particularly the poor and the deprived. As an Education Report submitted in the U.K. recorded: The best of schools must be in the worst of localities.

Pandit Jawaharlal Nehru said long ago: "It is science alone that can solve the problem of hunger and poverty. The future belongs to science and to those who make friends with science." Nobel Prize winner, Sir C.V. Raman records: "There is only one solution for India's economic problems and that is science, and more science and still more science."

We seem to be doing science, and yet poverty and ignorance do not seem to be leaving us. India has gone too fast to acquire modern technologies, while sacrificing possible ways for improving the economic conditions of the average man. Instead for working for the present, we have chosen to work for spectacular results in the distant future.

Our educational system in India is totally outdated and needs serious efforts to improve it. Gandhi said long ago, '...the present mode of education is radically wrong from bottom to top,' and that still holds. Education is strongly dependent on the geographical and social environment and therefore copying the systems developed elsewhere will not work. We can learn from work done and experience gained abroad, but it will have to be adapted to suit our cultural background. We will have to work hard to evolve a new and democratic educational system, if it has to help in the progress of the country, both in science and ethics.

The present book has been divided into three parts. In Part I we present our views on Science and Truth, and on Religion and Truth. On Science and Truth we have relied heavily on our discussions with and the writings of Professor D.S. Kothari. On Religion and Truth we have tried to present the views mainly of Gandhi.

We begin Part II by a brief biographical note on the late Professor D.S. Kothari. It is followed by some articles/papers and reviews that have already been published, but which are highly relevant. These include a paper published by D.S. Kothari in Science and Culture to explain the principle of complementarity at a very elementary level in terms of a conversation between a classical physicist and a modern physicist. The concept of identity and non-identity as explained by Lord Buddha to his disciples is also included, for it can greatly help in our understanding of similar concepts in modern physics. Some excerpts from Schroedinger's book 'My View of the World' are also included.

Dr. Kothari wrote a book on 'Nuclear Explosions and Their Effects', which was published in 1958 by Government of India. It was translated into many foreign languages and has been described as a 'history making book'. Its conclusion are still relevant and we reproduce them here with slight modifications.

D.S. Kothari Centre for Science, Ethics and Education has recently brought out Collections of his Lectures, Convocation Addresses, Memorial lectures etc. Reviews of these four books are included at the end of Part II of the book.

In Part III we reproduce a few lectures/articles of Prof. D.S. Kothari, after minor editing. These are:

1. Science and Human Progress (Inaugural Address at 32nd Annual Meeting of the National Academy of Science, Allahabad, 16th February 1963)

This address, though delivered in 1963, is still relevant. Science is vital for the progress of any country, but the final outcome depends upon how it is used. Therefore correct and proper planning of the use of science, which is dependent on the policies of the Government of the country, requires great thought and commitment.

2. Science and Man's Future (National Academy of Science, Annual Session, Ujjain, 26th February 1971)

In this lecture Dr. Kothari emphasises the need for man to understand himself. Science is advancing rapidly but to survive in this Atomic Age, man must understand himself. Dr. Kothari explains how chemical and physical laws are exactly the same whether we deal with animate or with inanimate things. Science deals with the external objective world. It cannot deal with the inner world of subjective experience. However quantum mechanics leads to consciousness, and this aspect has been explained in detail.

3. Science and Vedant (Bhavan's Journal 29 (1) pp. 1-5, 1982)

The most significant and basic characteristic of science is its objectivity. It is also universal. Science excludes subjectivity. Brain is objective while mind is subjective. Yet mind influences brain and *vice versa*. Science provides no answer to this great riddle. One has to look into the Vedas to get some understanding of this riddle. Dr. Kothari discusses this at some length in this article.

4. Science and Values (Proc. Golden Jubilee Celebrations, INSA, New Delhi, pp. 123-133, 1984)

In this article Dr. Kothari emphasises and explains the complementarity of science and moral values. He writes that 'man has now reached a stage in evolution when his survival and future evolution is possible only on the basis of Science and *Ahimsa*'. Science properly taught can contribute much to the incorporation of moral component in education.

5. S-T and Concern for the People (Proc. Indian Natn. Sci. Acad. 56, No.2 pp. 137-144, 1990)

Science must think in terms of millions and billions of people. The key issue in national development is how to join Science and Technology (S and T) with concern for the well being and advancement of all people, particularly the poor ones. He regrets that nearly all S-T development is directed to means for men to kill one another, and almost nothing for men to love one another. He argues that science and science education have a crucial role to play to eliminate suffering and reduce the widening gap between the rich and the poor countries and between the rich and the poor within a country.

6. National Science Exhibition for Children–Welcome Address-14th November 1971

The first National Science Exhibition for Children was organised in 1971 on Pandit Jawaharlal Nehru's birthday and was inaugurated by the then President of India, Shri V.V. Giri. In his Welcome Address, Dr. Kothari stated that the purpose of the Exhibition was to promote science education and dissemination of science. It was to encourage co-operative effort between students and teachers, and reinforce initiative, innovation and creativity.

These exhibitions are regularly being organised every year since then.

2

Science and Truth

I. Concept of Truth in Science and Ethics

Gandhi said: "My uniform experience has convinced me that there is no other God than Truth." All our ethic rests on truth, so do science and mathematics. But the meaning of truth is quite different in all these three fields.

What is truth? If we look up Oxford Dictionary, we find 'Truth' is defined as: "being true; loyalty, accuracy, integrity, etc.; that which is true, true statement, 'account', belief, etc.; reality, fact." We now look up the words 'loyalty', 'accuracy', and all the rest that are supposed to give the meaning of the word truth. We soon realise that we can know what 'truth' is if we know what 'reality' is; and what 'reality' is if we know what 'existence' is; and what 'existence' is if we know what 'fact' is. We are back to the starting point. As such a dictionary is of little use for defining 'truth'.

Yet every one of us can intuitively distinguish between truth and untruth, at least in most cases. We observe nature through our five senses, those of sight, sound, smell, touch and taste.

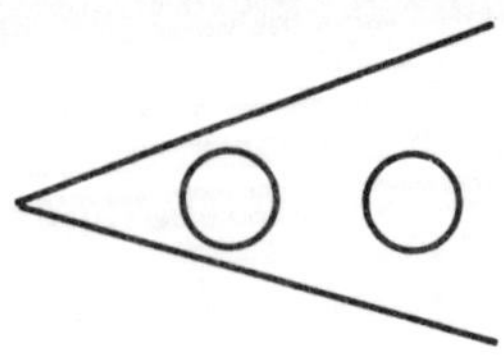

Fig. 1

When we observe an object or hear a sound, our mind forms a

picture. Our experience tells us that normally the picture formed is correct, as we can compare that with what someone else observing the same thing describes. However, occasionally our senses can mislead us. For example, a colour-blind person does not quite see things the way a normal person does.

Or consider figure 1. The two circles are of exactly the same size, yet the one on the left appears bigger. In this case our sense of sight misleads us. Similarly the segment *ab* is equal to *bc*, but segment *bc* appear longer (Fig. 2). In everyday life we have to rely on our senses and what we learn from them, we take as the truth.

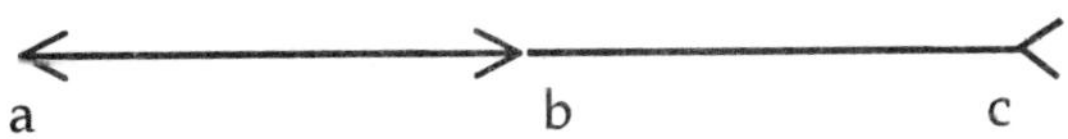

Fig. 2

When we deal with extremely small objects like molecules and atoms, then our senses are of no help. Some of the laws of nature deduced from our careful observation of the world around us, break down for the microscopic world. Even our intuition fails there and we find major contradictions with our common sense. The atomic concept provides an example of profound historical significance. So long as it is an intuitive concept — that is, an atom is pictured as an extremely small ball — the atom can be imagined to be divisible into parts, and these into still smaller parts and so on till its elements vanish into "nothing" There is no escape from this logical contradiction, and this is why the atomic concept was rejected by Vedantic and Buddhist thinkers. The way out of the difficulty has proved to be totally unexpected. It took more than a thousand years. The discovery of the quantum of action has shown that the atomic concept is not *intuitive — an atom is not a "small ball"*. An atom is both *indivisible* and *divisible* and it involves no contradiction because of the *non-intuitive* nature of the concept.

Let us begin by considering what we mean by truth in mathematics, because this is the simplest of all.

Mathematical Truth

Mathematics is usually thought of as a boring subject dealing with long and tedious calculations pertaining mainly to business or banking or filling income tax forms. Few realise that it is a jewel of human knowledge. Ramanujam spent his whole life thinking and writing mathematics. He died in 1920 at a young age of 32 years, leaving behind three notebooks full of mathematical notes which experts are still trying to decipher. A fourth 'lost' notebook was discovered in 1976 and even this contains a large number of highly significant results and formulae.

Some individuals are able to devote their entire life to mathematics because they have discovered its beauty and joy. As the great mathematician G.H. Hardy (supervisor and co-worker of Ramanujam at Cambridge University) wrote: "The mathematician's patterns, like the painter's or the poet's, must be beautiful; the ideas like the colours or words, must fit together in a harmonious way. Beauty is the first test, there is no permanent place in the world for ugly mathematics.... It may be very hard to define mathematical beauty, but that is just as true of beauty of any kind." He further wrote, "If his (mathematician's) patterns are more permanent than theirs (painter's and poet's), it is because they are made with 'ideas'."

A point under debate since long is whether one discovers mathematics or just creates it. In other words, are mathematical truths already there and we do not know them until someone discovers them, or do we create mathematics?

Mathematicians enjoy studying things that seem utterly useless, just for the fun of it. It may only be centuries later that some use is found of these studies. Ancient Greeks studied non-circular curves — ellipse, parabola and hyperbola, which we now know as conic sections. (Conics are curves that are obtained by taking a suitable section of a single or double cone.) The first important applications of these curves were found in the 17th century. Kepler discovered that planets move round the sun in elliptical orbits and Galileo found that when we throw any object up at an angle, it follows a parabolic path. In the 19th century Riemann generalised Euclid's geometry for curved surfaces. Even a "straight line" had to be defined again and most of Euclid's theorems were reformulated. Einstein's General Theory of Relativity (around 1916) could be developed only because of Riemann's earlier contributions.

A mathematical theory starts with a small number of axioms and undefined terms. The truth of the axioms and the meaning of the undefined terms is assumed to be known intuitively. It is not open to question or further investigation within the framework of that theory. The development of the theory consists in proving new theorems on the basis of axioms and theorems already proved. The new theorems unless trivial, are first 'discovered' and then proved. Discovery is an inspired guess, a flash of insight. The theorems are true. The question whether a mathematical truth has a scientific or physical relevance is outside mathematics.

As a simple example let us consider the following theorem of geometry: the sum of the three angles of any triangle is always equal to two right angles. If one tries to verify this theorem by actual measurement, that is impossible, since all measurements are limited by observational errors which can never be eliminated. Even a straight line drawn on a sheet of paper must have a certain width to be visible, but a geometrical line has no width — it is one-dimensional. Further, we have no means of knowing whether the scale used to draw the line is straight — ideally. Thus mathematical truths are based on reason alone. In contrast, scientific truths are based on experience. The two are different, but they do not work in isolation. They are related to each other as *mind* and *matter* are related. Mind can conceive of any number of dimensions, but the experience of the external world leads us to conceive the physical world around us as three-dimensional. Einstein needed four dimensions to develop his special theory of Relativity.

We must remember that if we want to understand nature — 'talk' to nature — the only language it understands is mathematics. Whether it is inanimate matter or animate beings, they are all bound by the same laws of nature, which can be precisely stated only in mathematical form. A deep study of mathematics is essential to understand ourselves and the world around us.

One of the great wonders of nature is that it follows the laws of mathematics. One can precisely describe its behaviour in minutest detail in terms of mathematical equations. As we shall see a little later, we can neither comprehend the dual nature of light nor of electrons: we face striking contradictions when we try to physically understand either of them. Yet, both of these, light as well as electrons — can be precisely and correctly described in term of mathematics.

Thus mathematical truths are the most profound truths. They tell us what is possible and what is not. In some sense they are eternal; quite unlike scientific truths, which get modified by future developments. As Heinrich Hertz put it: 'One cannot escape the feeling that these mathematical formulae have an independent existence and an intelligence of their own, that they are even wiser than their discoverers, that we get more out of these than was originally put into them.'

Theories in Science

In science, both theory and experiment play important roles. They go hand in hand. An experiment is designed to test some specific theoretical result or prediction, and if the experimental results disagree with the theory, it is time to improve the theory. Improvement of theory is a continuing process resulting from a continuous confrontation with experiment. In science a theory is always tentative, waiting to be replaced by an improved and more comprehensive theory. A successful theory helps in the advancement of knowledge by suggesting new problems and experiments. A good theory is a guide to its own replacement — it is always provisional.

Newton developed the theory of gravitation around 1666 and it held sway for over three hundred years. With the help of a few postulates he was able to explain the motion of planets around the sun and the motion of moons (satellites) around the planets. One could predict both solar and lunar eclipses years in advance, as well as understand ocean tides. Apart from all this, Newton's theory had a tremendous philosophical impact on man's thinking. It was realised for the first time that laws of nature discovered by man on the earth had universal validity — they applied to the entire universe.

Over the years, it was observed that planet mercury — the one closest to the sun, showed small departures from Newton's theory. People tried to explain it in various ways, but it was left to Einstein to formulate a completely new theory of gravitation in 1916. It not only succeeded in explaining the motion of planet Mercury but also predicted that light rays would slightly bend when passing close to a star. This new and totally unexpected behaviour of light was experimentally verified in 1919. Newton's theory is not wrong, it is a special case of Einstein's theory.

Search for truths about nature is science. It is a creative activity. When one obtains a new insight into the working of nature, one is as much thrilled as say a painter or a sculptor when he creates a masterpiece. However, there is one major difference between science and the arts. Scientific effort is cumulative and co-operative, whereas each artistic creation is complete in itself. In science, every newly established fact, however insignificant it may appear to be at the time, and every new idea, however small, is bound sooner or later to contribute to major advances in our understanding of nature. Even such a great physicist as Newton wrote: 'If I can see a little farther, it is by standing on the shoulders of giants.'

Pursuit of science is one of the most selfless human activities. There are many branches of science, such as astronomy, cosmology, high energy particle physics, parts of geophysics, which are pursued with great devotion and in which enormous amount of money is spent, which have no possible applications as far as one can see. There have been people who have spent their entire life studying some very restricted aspect of nature, just watching birds for example or observing stars at night. This total commitment to a chosen field is not peculiar to men of science. We find this in saints, and in all great artists, musicians, writers and others. One cannot define their motivation: in some sense it is service to God. As Einstein put it, 'The state of the mind that enables a man to do work of this kind is akin to that of the religious worshipper or the lover: the daily effort comes from no deliberate intentions or programme, but straight from the heart.'

Study of nature is capable of transforming us, of helping us to become ourselves — human beings. Henri Poincare, the great French Philosopher and Mathematician says: 'He who has tasted of this (something which is greater than ourselves..... it is a joy in which we forget ourselves and thus it is morally sound), who has seen, if only from afar, the splendid harmony of the natural laws, will be better disposed than another to pay little attention to his petty, egoistic interests. He will have an ideal, which he will value more than himself, and that is the only ground on which we can build an ethics. He will work for this ideal without sparing himself and without expecting any of those regular rewards which are everything to persons ...

'It is the love of truth even more than passion, which inspires him. And is not such a love an entire code of morality.'

Science helps us to identify what is possible. It liberates us from superstition, magic and sorcery. For example, a bird sitting on the branch of a tree is what it appears to be and not a witch who has assumed this form, nor some human being under a magic spell. Science helps to strengthen our faith in reason and warns us against anti-reason. However, science admits that there is a whole different world where it has no say, it is beyond science. One must realise this very important distinction between beyond – science and anti-science. Anti-science or anti-reason should have no place in our lives. Our faith in science is itself not a part of science — it is beyond science (it is not anti-science). To suffer for the sake of science and truth, as many scientists, including Galileo, have done is beyond science — it is a moral quality. Paradoxically, though reason and faith appear to be opposed to each other, they sustain and reinforce each other beyond measure.

II. Science and the External Objective World

Among the sciences, physics is the simplest since it deals with matter, its constituents and energy. This also accounts for the fact that progress of science has been rapid and phenomenal. It is interesting to recall that towards the end of the nineteenth century scientists were of the view that all laws of nature had been discovered and what was left for future scientists was only 'to improve the decimal point', *i.e.* improve the precision of measurement of various physical quantities. 'Classical physics', *i.e.* physics prior to the 20th century, could easily be comprehended by all since it was close to man's daily experience. For example, Newton's great contributions to the study of motion and gravitation present no difficulty in our understanding them.*

This situation changed radically during the first decade of the 20th century. Now scientists realise that they know enough about nature to be able to say that we do not understand nature.

Let us consider a few simple examples to get some idea of the mysteries of nature.

We start by examining the most abundant substance on the surface of the earth: water. It is a miracle, whichever way you look at it. Most substances contract when they cool and solidify. Water has the highest density at 4°C and expands when it turns into ice and therefore becomes lighter. That is why ice floats on water. If ice did not float, all oceans would have frozen solid ages ago and only a little water would have been available on the top. Under such conditions life could not have evolved. Also since ice is lighter than water, life survives inside lakes and oceans in cold climates. Water can dissolve considerable amount of oxygen and allows fish and other life forms to breath inside water. It can also dissolve a large number of different salts and for this reason it is the main constituent of all living forms. It has the highest specific heat and this helps to keep our body temperature steady. It has the largest latent heat of vaporisation. Because of this, during scorching heat, evaporation of water from our body surface keeps us cool. Trees also keep cool because of evaporation of water from their leaves — and that is why they get new leaves just before summer.

---

* We say that the concepts in classical physics are anthropomorphic, *i.e.* they conform to reality as observed by our sense organs.

Apart from all this, water forms beautiful crystals with varied shapes. No two crystals have the same shape, they seem to reflect the variety of forms we humans have. But the most striking thing is that we still do not fully understand the behaviour of water. In a recent research paper published in the international journal 'Science', the author writes: 'Despite decades of extensive investigations into the properties of water and its chemical behaviour, there remain important unanswered questions that may have significant import on many chemical and biological problems.'

Almost 99.99 per cent of all living matter is composed of four of the 92 naturally occurring elements. These are hydrogen, carbon, nitrogen and oxygen. As we know, an atom of each element is composed of a positively charged nucleus with negatively charged electrons going around it. In an atom of oxygen, the nucleus consists of 8 protons and 8 neutrons and its size is roughly 5×10^{-15}m. Since oxygen atom, in its normal state, is electrically neutral, there are 8 electrons going round the nucleus in different orbits. The size of an atom is about 10^{-10} m. If we were to build a scale model of an atom, with the nucleus being of the size of a pinhead, the atom would be a sphere of diameter of almost 20 m. Thus we see that atoms are essentially all empty space, very much like our solar system. Then how is it that we can stand on the ground and it does not give way?

We are born, live and die on the surface of the earth. Do we have any relationship with the universe-with the stars? Yes, we are a part of the universe and the elements out of which our bodies are composed were 'cooked' inside the stars. Billions of years ago some stars exploded as they do even now, and scattered the debris all around. Some of it collected to form planets and in rare cases life evolved. Thus we owe our very existence to some distant stars, which may now be no more.

Life evolved and exists on the surface of the earth because of the sun. Sunlight is essential both for plants and animals. Properties of sunlight as well as of the light emitted by stars had been studied by physicists for long. By the end of the 19th century lot of empirical data was available and scientists had discovered quite a few 'laws' to describe certain specific properties of the emitted radiation. Inspite of this, a clear and unified understanding of all the different laws was missing.

Maxwell formulated four equations (now known as Maxwell's equations) to correctly describe propagation of light waves. He showed that these are electromagnetic in nature and similar to X-rays, microwaves, radio waves etc. This was a very major advance in our understanding of electromagnetic waves. Light waves show interference and diffraction just like waves on any water surface. Colour of soap films or of oil films on water surface is due to interference of light waves. These days special plastic sheets are available, which people sometimes stick to the glass screen on the back of their cars, and which shine brightly showing different colours at different angles. These are a form of diffraction grating and diffract light. Again, people use sunglasses made of polaroids to avoid dazzle. All these confirm the wave nature of light. All radio and television broadcasts as well as telecommunication systems are based on the properties of electromagnetic waves.

At the beginning of the last century, to explain the properties of radiation emitted from hot bodies, the German physicist, Planck suggested that light must also behave like particles and he called them quanta. We now also refer to them as photons. Even Planck felt that his idea, though it somehow explained the observed results, was totally ridiculous. How could a wave behave like a particle? He described his suggestion 'as an act of despair'. Niels Bohr, talking about Planck wrote: 'In some sense it can be said that he used the last forty years of his life, not to say fifty, to try to get his discovery out of the world'. However, Einstein was a strong supporter of his idea and it was soon experimentally verified. It is interesting to recall that Einstein was awarded the Nobel Prize for his work on the quantum nature of light, though lot of his other work was equally if not much more revolutionary.

We see that light not only behaves as waves, but also as particles. When we look for its wave properties, it appears as a wave and when we look for its particle properties it appears as particles. Einstein said: "All these 50 years of conscious brooding have brought me no nearer to the answer to the question 'what are light quanta?' Now-a-days every Tom, Dick and Harry thinks he knows it, but he is mistaken."

We find that towards the beginning of the last century, our understanding of nature changed radically. Earlier it was believed that what we observed with our senses was the Truth and scientists discovered many laws of nature, based on such observations. It is said that Newton discovered the law of gravitation by observing an apple falling from an apple tree. Earlier Galileo discovered the law of the pendulum by observing the oscillations of a chandelier hanging in a cathedral. Even when we see a huge aeroplane flying it appears reasonable, since it is directly or indirectly connected with our everyday experience — we have all seen birds flying.

When scientists began to study nature on a microscopic scale, they were greatly surprised to find that certain phenomena did not at all tally with their earlier experience. They realised that certain laws that they had discovered on the macroscopic scale had to be totally modified when dealing with nature at the atomic scale. Should it therefore surprise us if we find that the laws or truths about Mind are not comprehensible in terms of our experience of the external world?

We have already considred the duel nature of light. Let us now consider another case of the microscopic world.

Let us consider matter. Electrons are a basic constituent of all matter. They are responsible for transporting electrical energy. The beautiful coloured images seen on our television sets are formed by beam of electrons falling on the screen. (You can test this by bringing a small magnet close to the screen and the image will get distorted near the magnet.) Scientists have measured the charge and the mass of an electron with fantastic accuracy. The mass of an electron is $9.1093897 \times 10^{-31}$ kg and its charge is $-1.60217733 \times 10^{-19}$ coulomb. These quantities are known with an accuracy better than one part in a million. It is like measuring the length of a large hall with an accuracy of one hundredth of a millimetre.

It has been observed that under certain conditions, these same particles whose charge and mass have been so precisely measured, can behave as waves! Electron microscopes, which have a much higher resolving power than ordinary microscopes, are based on the wave nature of electrons. In other words, 'electrons' can behave both as particles or as waves, depending upon which aspect we are trying to observe. Thus, inspite of extensive studies on different aspects of electrons we are forced to conclude that we do not know what electrons are. In an interesting article written in the form of a conversation between a classical physicist and a quantum theorist, Dr. Kothari has tried to explain the meaning of the dual nature of particles in simple terms and how it differs from, say, observing two sides of a coin. (It is reproduced in the Second Part of the Book).

We find that if we think a little deeply we neither understand what is light nor what is matter. There is no word in the English language or for that matter in any language, to describe something which exhibits such mutually exclusive properties as those of a particle and a wave. A particle is totally localised in space at a given time. It possesses a definite mass and one can precisely find its velocity or speed at any given instant. On the other hand, at any given time a wave extends over all space. We characterise it by wavelength, frequency and amplitude. Thus in quantum science we seek 'reconciliation between uncompromising extremes.'

We see that both electrons and light can show both particle and wave properties. We say that the wave and the particle aspects are complementary and not contradictory. This also provides us with a criterion to distinguish between 'big' and 'small' objects. New physics provides an absolute meaning to these words. An object is small in the absolute sense if the effect of the disturbance that inevitably accompanies an act of observation is not negligible. A certain indeterminate disturbance is inevitable even under ideal conditions, that is, observations made with 'perfect instruments' supposed to be free from all limitations except those which are inherent in the very nature of things. If the disturbance produced due to observation has negligible effect on the state of the object, the object is said to be big in the absolute sense.

The principle of Complementarity that we owe principally

to Niels Bohr is perhaps the most significant and revolutionary concept of modern physics. Philosophically, it should be noted, it is very close to the Indian concept of Syadvada introduced by Jain and Buddhist thinkers more than two thousand years ago. Bohr had great faith in the future role in human affairs of the practical philosophy of complementarity. It can enable people to see that seemingly irreconcilable points of view need not be contradictory. These, on deeper understanding, may be found to be complementary and mutually illuminating — the two opposing, contradictory aspects being parts of a 'totality', seen from different perspectives. The complementarity approach allows the possibility of accommodating widely divergent human experiences into an underlying harmony, and bringing to light new social and ethical vistas for exploration and for alleviation of human suffering. Bohr fervently hoped that one day *complementarity* would be an integral part of everyone's education and provide guidance in the problems and challenges of life. For Bohr the complementarity approach that generated one of the greatest revolutions in natural philosophy was also of the utmost relevance for every aspect of man's life.

Apart from exhibiting both wave and particle properties, 'small' (in the absolute sense) objects exhibit other fantastic properties. If we want to simultaneously measure precisely the position and velocity of an electron, it cannot be done. However, sophisticated instruments we may devise, one can never do this, but this is not so far large objects. The different experimental set-up required for the measurement of different variables can, in principle, be joined together into one comprehensive apparatus. This one apparatus will measure everything measurable in principle for a big object. There is no objection to this procedure, because observations do not disturb the state of a big object under observation: All possible measurements can be made without interfering with each other with the aid of a single super instrument. But this is impossible for a small object. Why? The measurement of one variable for a small system, because of the non-negligible accompanying disturbance, disturbs the values of the other variables to be subsequently measured. We must, therefore, make a definite choice as to what variable we desire to measure for the system. For example: The set-up required for the measurement of position of an electron and that required for a measurement of velocity can, in no circumstances, be combined into a single super-instrument. This led Heisenberg to formulate his famous 'principle of uncertainty'. According to this principle both position and speed of a particle cannot simultaneously be measured precisely. If we want to measure, say the exact position of an electron through an ideal microscope, the act of observation, that is the scattering of light by the electron, will impart to the electron some uncertain amount of energy (and momentum) so that we would have no means of knowing what its speed was. Similarly if we use an instrument to precisely measure the speed of the electron, then we will not be able to locate its position precisely.

An all comprehensive instrument is impossible in quantum mechanics; because, in general, measurements are not compatible with one another for small objects. It is important to grasp this radically new situation.

Think of two identical particles. If these are to be absolutely identical, it should not be permissible to precisely define their trajectories, for otherwise their separate trajectories could be used to distinguish one particle from the other for all time — one particle riding one trajectory and the other a different one. Absolute identity of particles demands that there cannot exist for them sharply defined trajectories. This leads to the wave aspect; and hence the wave-particle duality.

It is essential to appreciate the absolute identity of all electrons in order to understand the chemistry of elements and the formation of compounds. Electrons in the body of A may appear to be different from those in the body of B; but this is an approximation we make for our convenience to understand the functioning of each individual. Correctly, all electrons in the universe have submerged themselves, as it were, in one 'brotherhood' of electrons. The 'Many' have become "One".

Another revolutionary concept was introduced in science by Einstein in the beginning of the 20th century. For centuries students were taught that in all activities, whether physical, chemical or biological, mass is conserved and so is energy. For example, if we drop a ball, it gains in speed as it falls. We know that this increase in its kinetic energy — the energy of motion, is at the expense of its decreasing potential energy — energy due to its having been moved up against the pull of the earth. At all time, its total energy, *i.e.* the sum of its kinetic energy and its potential energy, remains the same.

In every chemical reaction, whether simple or complex, the total mass of each material involved remains the same. For example, if we consider the formation of water by the combination of hydrogen and oxygen, then the total mass of say, oxygen, before the reaction would be the same as after the reaction.

In 1905 Einstein discovered his now famous equation

$$E = mc^2$$

where E is the energy equivalent of mass m and c is the velocity of light. He established the equivalence between mass and energy, and opened up the possibility of utilising the energy of the nuclei of atoms. Soon his theory was confirmed by experiments. Scientists were able to demonstrate experimentally that under suitable conditions energy (γ-rays) could be changed into matter (electron-positron pair) and matter (electron and positron pair) could be annihilated totally to create energy (γ-rays). Atom bombs, atomic power stations are a direct outcome of Einstein's equation. If 1 gram of uranium undergoes fission, the energy released will be almost equal to the energy generated by burning 1 ton of coal! The invention of atom bombs changed the course of world history. On the request of Pandit Nehru, Dr. Kothari wrote a book on 'Nuclear Explosions and Their Effects', which was published by the Government of India in 1956 (second edition appeared in 1958). It was translated in several world languages and described as 'a work...which makes history.' The conclusions drawn in the book are still relevant and partly reproduced in the Second Part of this Book.

Thanks to Einstein, we no longer have two laws of conservation, one for mass and another for energy, but only one for mass and energy.

We see that with advancement of science, definition of truth in science has also changed with time. In the beginning what was thought reasonable was the Truth. Aristotle (384-332 B.C.) said that heavier bodies fall faster than lighter ones, when dropped from a height. According to him any logically founded physical statement did not need any experimental proof. Only in the sixteenth century, Galileo demonstrated that all bodies, irrespective of their mass, fall under gravity at the same rate. He is remembered as the scientist who introduced experiments in science.

Sense of reasonableness also evolved with new discoveries. One knows that iron sinks in water, but steel ships float. Only when one understands Archimedes principle can one understand and explain the floating of ships. Similarly, one can understand the flying of aeroplanes, once one knows the related laws of physics.

But when we come to modern physics, and deal with 'small' particles or light, our imagination fails to reconcile with facts. As Dirac put it: "The new theories, if one looks apart from their mathematical setting, are built up from physical concepts which cannot be explained in terms of things previously known to the student, which cannot even be explained adequately in words at all. Like the fundamental concepts (*e.g.* proximity, identity) which everyone must learn on his arrival into this world, the newer concepts of physics can be mastered only by long familiarity with their properties and uses."

We need no reminding that, to begin with, all experience is subjective. How then objective knowledge becomes possible? All experience, everything without exceptions, is fundamentally a personal, subjective experience. When you and I look at a tree, there is no conceivable way of determining that my sensation of "green" is the same as yours. That your perception and mine of a given thing is identical has no clear, no objective, meaning. The basic point is that an objective statement is not, and cannot be about one single sense impression (say, my sensation of red colour produced by a flower), but it expresses always some relation between two sense impressions. My sense impression of red may be or may not be (who knows?) different from yours, but irrespective of this we can verify whether two given flowers are of red colour or they are not. This simple example can be readily generalised. The essence of the matter is that objective, communicable statements become possible about pairs of sense impressions — not about single sense impressions. It is this, which eliminates subjectivity, eliminates "I", and is the basis of the objectivity of science. "The fact that by comparing pairs communicable, objective statements are possible, has an immense importance because it is the root of speaking and writing, and of the most powerful instrument of thinking, of mathematics." (Max Born, My Life and My Views, 1968, Chapter Five, "Symbol and Reality," p. 174)

The objectivity of science makes it truly a co-operative enterprise, which can be shared by all men. Dogmatism of any kind whatsoever is totally inadmissible in science. Dogmatism is subjective. Its ultimate basis is personal prejudice or belief, not reason. Dogma is personal, science is public. Dogmatism and objectivity are a flagrant contradiction. The co-operative enterprise of science, thanks to its objectivity, has been astonishingly successful, perhaps far more than any other enterprise of man.

In dealing with atomic objects, we face a totally novel situation, which it is almost impossible to describe adequately in words without using the abstract language of mathematics. And there is something more to this very puzzling and tantalising situation. Several of the great physicists — but not all — who have given serious thought to the subject are of the view that an explicit involvement of consciousness is an essential factor in the act of observation. And consciousness plays a definite, not negligible, role in the process of influencing unpredictably the state of the observed atomic system. In the oft quoted words of E.P. Wigner: "The measurement is not complete until its result enters our consciousness...(This) last step is, at the present state of our knowledge, shrouded in mystery and no explanation has been given for it so far in terms of quantum mechanics, or in terms of any other theory."

Let us consider a specific example. We consider diffraction of neutrons by a very narrow slit (93 μm wide). The diffraction pattern observed is shown in Fig 3. Where in this pattern a given neutron will land, cannot be predicted. Quantum theory can only tell us the chance or the probability of a neutron landing at a particular spot. The question then is what decides where a given neutron will actually land? John von Neumann, a great physicist and mathematician, advocated that whatever was responsible for choosing the outcome of a measurement had to be something outside quantum theory and therefore outside physics itself. One has therefore to introduce consciousness into the physical world. As Eugene Wigner said: "The very study of the external world led to the conclusion that the content of the consciousness is an ultimate reality."

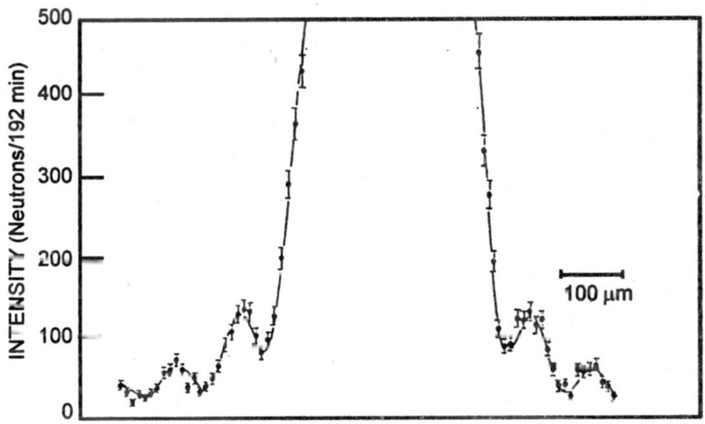

Fig. 3

III. Inner World — The Subjective World

When we visit a magic show we are thrilled to watch a rabbit being pulled out of a hat, or objects, including human beings, floating in mid air. We wonder how such magic is performed and may discuss this with friends for days. These are all tricks performed to entertain people. Though one may not be able to explain any particular trick, it is certain that it cannot violate any laws of nature. What we do not realise is that the magician's show is nothing compared to what Nature shows us everyday at every step. Even a common fly or an ant can do things of wonder if we ponder a little. How do these small things see, smell, move around, even fly, eat, reproduce and bring up their progeny? But even a greater wonder is, what scientists refer to as, the brain-mind problem or the matter-mind problem.

Let us consider an example. When you read this chapter, light from different sources falls on the page and is scattered. The scattered light reaches your eyes. An inverted and highly reduced image is formed on the retina. This induces electrical signals, which travel to certain parts of the brain. In the brain there are only electrical signals and nothing else. Then, how is it that you can read and understand what is written on the page? How are electrical signals, which are material in nature, transformed into images and thoughts, which are non-material? Or stated conversely, how do our thoughts and feelings, which are no-material influence our body, which is material. When you think of turning a page, how is it that the hand moves and performs the required task? At present this is a complete mystery and is beyond the scope of science. As Sir Charles Sherrington, writes: 'thoughts, feelings and so on are not amenable to the energy-matter concept. They lie outside it. Therefore they lie outside Natural Science...'

It is thus important to realise that there are many things beyond science. This is not the same as anti-science. Anything anti-science should be totally unacceptable. All laws of nature are space and time invariant, *i.e.* they hold everywhere in space, and both in the past and the future. If a law of nature is broken at a particular place at any particular time, the law will become invalid for all times.

Some years ago, 'Nature', one of the world's leading science journals published an Editorial under the title 'Don't scoff at miracles'. It cited some cases of terminally sick persons, who later recovered completely. Recently a very senior neurosurgeon related an incident of an old lady who was in the last stage of her life. She was not expected to live beyond a couple of months. The doctors asked her son to take the lady home. To console the lady, they told her that she was now well and should go to Haridwar and lead a peaceful life, worshipping God. After about a year the lady, along with her son, came to the Hospital to meet the neurosurgeon. She introduced herself and thanked the doctors for the advice and help she had received. The doctors were greatly surprised to see her. On checking her condition, they found her hale and hearty. They considered this as nothing short of a miracle.

Science is the causal way of looking at things. It answers only the question 'Why' but never the question *to what end or to what purpose*? It deals with what is possible and can be done, but not with what ought to be done. Einstein says: ".... if someone asks 'To what purpose should we help one another, make life easier for each other, make beautiful music or have inspired thoughts?' he should have to be told: 'If you don't feel it, no one can explain it to you.' Without this primary feeling we are nothing and had better not live at all."

There are two distinct realities: the 'external world' which we see around us and the 'inner world' of the mind or the self. Science deals with the external world of space and time, matter and energy. Religion or Dharma deals with the internal world, the world of values. *Science is the basis of technology while religion is the basis of ethics*. Science can help in increasing production of food and other items, but ethics has to come in for their equitable distribution.

Thus there are two important things. Firstly, *the duality of the two worlds*, and secondly *the question of interaction between them*. The 'external world' and the 'inner world', that is to say, the 'atom' and the 'self' should be accepted as equally significant for human life. They are both equally real. Cyril Hinshelwood observes: "To deny the reality of the inner world is a flat negation of all that is immediate in existence; to minimise its significance is to depreciate the very purpose of living, and to explain it away as a product of natural science is plain fallacy."

Another great biologist, Penfield writes: "Throughout my scientific career, I, like other scientists, have struggled to prove that the brain accounts for the mind. But now, perhaps, the time has come when we may profitably consider the evidence as it stands, and ask the question: Do brain mechanisms account for the mind?" And he concludes: "Because it seems to me certain that it will always be quite impossible to explain the mind on the basis of neuronal action within the brain, and because it seems to me that the mind develops and matures independently throughout an individual's life as though it were a continuing element.... I am forced to choose the proposition that our being is to be explained on the basis of two fundamental elements."

Objective science by excluding subjectivity cannot, even in principle, deal with our thoughts, feelings, and emotions, with subjective experience of any kind. It excludes "I". The exclusion is total. Our feelings of pain, joy, ecstasy, and what not are inherently incapable of unambiguous communication. Even if I succeed in expressing in words some particular feeling or emotional state of mine, there is no proof — there can be no proof — that my words will produce within you feelings identical to mine. Consciousness, mind, soul, "I", or whatever name we may give to subjectivity, or to any aspect of it, has no place in natural science. No considerations of purpose, divine or human, nothing which implies value judgements, can enter the gateway of objective science.

It is apparent that the basic distinction between brain and mind is all important. Brain is a part of the objective world. It can be investigated objectively; and recent developments in molecular biology have given valuable knowledge of its structure and functioning. On the other hand, mind is subjective. When, for instance, sound waves impinge on our ears, the pressure changes produce electric currents in the nerve fibres which reach the brain. How do these electric currents in the brain transform in the mind into sensations of sound-into music? The same applies to other sensations. Science provides no answer to this riddle. Because of its very objectivity science can give no answer to this riddle of all riddles. To quote Sir Charles Sherrington [*Man on his Nature*. Cambridge University Press (1951), pp. 228-257]: "The mental is not examinable as a form of energy. That in brief is the gap which parts psychiatry with physiology.... Thoughts, feelings and so on are not amenable to energy (matter) concept. They lie outside it. Therefore they lie outside Natural Science.... In some ways this is embarrassing for biology. Biology as its name says is the study of life.... Natural science has studied life to the extent of explaining away life as any radically separable category of phenomena.... there is no radical scientific difference between living and dead.... But though living is analysable and describable by natural science, that associate of living, thought, escapes and remains refractory to natural science.... Our mental experience is not open to observation through any sense organ..... Mind, for anything perception can compass, goes therefore in our spatial world more ghostly than a ghost, invisible, intangible, it is a "thing" not even of outline, it is not a "thing". It remains without sensual confirmation, and remains without it for ever."

What about the *interaction* between the mind and the body? The control of the mind over the body is an incontrovertible fact of personal experience. If my mind, my thought, does not determine the movement of the pen in my hand, who is writing this sentence? Who is responsible for it? Equally, the influence of the body on the mind is incontrovertible as exemplified by effects of food and drugs, by neurological experiments, brain injuries, and so on. W. Penfield has recorded that in some striking cases of brain surgery when the patient was asked not to move the arm when the corresponding area of the cerebral cortex was electrically simulated, the patient invariable responded by using the other arm to hold it down. What the electrode did to one arm, the patient's will did to the other, concluded Penfield.

Even Einstein writes: "The most beautiful experience we can have is the mysterious. It is the fundamental emotion which stands at the cradle of true art and true science. Whoever does not know it and can no longer wonder, no longer marvel, is as good as dead, and his eyes are dimmed. It was the experience of mystery — even if mixed with fear — that engendered religion. A knowledge of the existence of something we cannot penetrate, our perceptions of the profoundest reason and the most radiant beauty, which only in their most primitive forms are accessible to our minds — it is this knowledge and this emotion that constitute true religiosity; in this sense, and in this alone, I am a deeply religious man. I cannot conceive of a God who rewards and punishes his creatures, or has a will of the kind that we experience in ourselves. Neither can I nor would I want to conceive of an individual that survives his physical death; let feeble souls, from fear or absurd egoism, cherish such thoughts. I am satisfied with the mystery of the eternity of life and with the awareness and a glimpse of the marvellous structure of the existing world, together with the devoted striving to comprehend a portion be it ever so tiny, of the Reason that manifests itself in nature".

Einstein firmly believed that there is *"a superior mind that reveals itself in the world of experience"*.

This observation is obviously very relevant for the mind-body problem. For centuries science and religion were considered as opposed to each other: one is based on logic and reason, and the other on faith. Only now we realise that they are not contradictory but complementary. Taken together they form the whole. As Einstein said: "Science is lame without religion, and religion is blind without science." The great mathematician and philosopher A.N. Whitehead observed: "It is no exaggeration to say that the future of civilisation depends on the degree to which we can balance the forces of science and religion."

IV. Reconciliation of the Two Worlds

The basis and strength of science is its objectivity. In science there is no role for purpose or goal. Yet the very decision to pursue science rather than anything else is a moral decision.

Science is objective but love of science is purely subjective. At first sight the objective world of science and the subjective world of personal experience or 'I' appear to be two entirely different worlds. The world of science has 'room for every thing, but none for man'. People carried away by the overwhelming success of science and technology tend to believe that what is not in science, does not exist.

One cannot prove the laws of ethics by any laws of science. They appear to be irreconcilable. For example, kindness is an universally accepted virtue, but in the words of Bertrand Russell: "No scientific explanation can be given as to why it is bad to inflict wanton cruelty on ones fellows ... Science by itself cannot supply us with ethics."

What we must recognise is that reality has many facets and science is just one of them. The different aspects of reality are complementary to one another and not contradictory. In his book, *What is Life*? (1949) Ervin Schrodinger writes:

> "So let us see whether we cannot draw the correct, non-contradictory conclusion from the following two premises:
>
> (*i*) My body functions as a pure mechanism according to the Laws of Nature.
> (*ii*) Yet I know, by incontrovertible direct experience, that I am directing its motions, of which I foresee the effects, that may be fateful and all-important, in which case I feel and take full responsibility for them.
>
> The only possible inference from these two facts is, I think, that I-I in the widest meaning of the word, that is to say, every conscious mind that has ever said or felt 'I'— am the person, if any, who controls the 'motion of the atoms' according to the "Laws of Nature".
>
> In itself, the insight is not new. The earliest records to my knowledge date back some 2,500 years or more. From the early great Upanishads the

> recognition ***Atman = Brahman*** (the personal self equals the omnipresent, all-comprehending eternal self) was in Indian thought considered, far from being blasphemous, to represent the quintessence of the deepest insight into the happenings of the world. The striving of all the scholars of Vedanta was, after having learnt to pronounce with their lips, really to assimilate in their minds this grandest of all thoughts."

To disregard the complementarity of scientific and ethical truths — the complementarity of matter and mind, of body and soul — can lead only to de-personalisation and de-humanisation of life. The highest type of scientific activity is not possible without a supreme faith in science and in man. This is a moral quality. There is no inherent contradiction in the same person being an intellectual giant and a spiritual pigmy, but in real life it is most unlikely. When asked (during a serious illness) whether he was at all afraid of death, Einstein said: "I feel such a sense of solidarity with all living things that it does not matter to me where the individual begins and ends". And he said, "There is nothing in the world, which I could not dispense with at a moment's notice". How close to Gandhi are the ethical convictions of Einstein! He regarded Gandhi as "the greatest man of the age".

The most significant lesson we can learn from the highly impressive and totally unexpected developments in physics in the last century is that we should not be misled by apparent contradictions, but try to understand the underlying complementarities. We owe this great lesson to Niels Bohr. The principle of complementarity is an expression of a totally novel and totally unexpected situation we confront in atomic phenomena. No longer it is possible, permissible, to make a sharp distinction between subject and object, between the knower and the thing to be known. If I look at my watch, my looking at it doesn't disturb or influence the time it indicates. I don't alter the position of the moon by looking at it. But this is not so when we deal with individual atomic events. An act of observation, even under ideal conditions, disturbs in some unforeseen way the thing to be observed. Such a situation — such interplay between subject and object, between the observer and what is being observed is wholly new to physics. But outside the exact sciences, it is commonplace. It occurs almost every moment. Take the interaction between a speaker and the audience. It is not like my looking at the moon. A speaker influences his audience — some are coaxed to sleep, and the audience influences him. He may feel encouraged or frightened depending on how the audience reacts.

The great Japanese physicist Yukawa whose prediction of Meson is a beautiful example of the application of complementarity to nuclear physics has remarked that the Japanese physicists did not feel the same difficulty as those in the West in adapting their thinking to the complementarity principle. "Bohr's argumentation has always appeared quite evident to us"; he says, and adding, "you see, we in Japan have not been corrupted by Aristotle". In a climate of Aristotelian logic and Platonic idealism the complementarity principle is not easy to grasp.

Our ancient Indian Philosophy emphasises at almost every step this principle of complementarity. Shri Aurbindo remarked that the principle followed by Upanishadic thought is to seek "reconciliation of uncompromising extremes." Consider, for examples Verses 4 and 5 of Isha Upanishad: Verse 4. One unmoving that is swifter than Mind. That the Gods reach not, for it progresses even in front. That, standing, passes beyond others as they run...., Verse 5. That moves and that moves not; that is far and the same is near; that is within all this and that also in outside all this.

In these verses, almost every sentence seems to contradict itself. How can something, which is not moving, be faster than the mind? To appreciate the meaning of these is not at all easy, because what the *rishis* tried to do was to convey their experiences to others through words. Spiritual experience is a part of the 'inner world' and language is a part of the 'external world' and as we have seen these two are complementary. One's experiences, particularly if they are deep and highly significant, cannot be correctly conveyed to others. There is unambiguous testimony for God realisation 'here and now' by seekers of the highest integrity and spiritual attainments in all ages and countries. The evidence is far too significant to be evaded or ignored. But this experience can never be conveyed to others truly and correctly.

There is another point we have to keep in mind. We have to distinguish between two kinds of truth, profound truths and trivial truths. For a profound truth its opposite or negation is also a profound truth. For a trivial truth its opposite is false, an absurdity. If one sees a chair and says that there is a chair — it would be a true statement. To say that it is not a chair would be false. But let us consider the statement 'There is a God', a statement of great wisdom and truth. Its converse 'There is no God' is also a statement of great wisdom and truth. For him who believes in no God, his God is 'no God', since the different aspects of God are infinite, inexhaustible, and inexpressible. This reminds one of the dialogue between Mahavira and his favourite disciple Gautama [Nathmal Tatia, *Studies in Jaina Philosophy* (1951), 22-23]:

> Are the souls, O Lord! eternal or non-eternal?
> The souls, O Gautama! are eternal in some respect and non-eternal in some respect.
> With what end in view, O Lord! is it said that the souls are eternal in some respect and non-eternal in some respect?
> They are eternal! O Gautama, from the viewpoint of substance, and non-eternal from the viewpoint of modes. And with this end in view it is said, O Gautama! that the souls are eternal in some respect and non-eternal in some respect.
> Is the body, O Lord! identical with the soul or is the body different from it?
> The body, O Gautama! is identical with the soul as well as it is different from it.

Even in the Gita we find such complementary statements. In Verse 61 of Chapter 18, Lord Krishna tells Arjun:

'The Lord dwells in the hearts of all beings, O Arjun and by his Maya causes all beings to revolve as though mounted on a machine.'

Yet, in Verse 63 he says,

'Thus has wisdom more profound than all profundities been declared to you by Me. Reflect upon it fully and act as you choose.'

How do we interpret the Lord asking Arjun to 'act as you choose', when earlier he proclaims that 'His Maya causes all beings to revolve as though mounted on a machine'?

The grand synthesis of 'action' (Karma Yoga) and 'renunciation' (Jnana Yoga) offered by the Gita is a masterly exposition of complementarity approach as a guide to human actions and aspirations.

Jain philosophy directly advocates complementarity. Syadvada (Syad means may be) was formulated probably more than two thousand years ago. Syadvada asserts that the knowledge of reality is possible only by denying the absolutist attitude. According to the Syadvada scheme every fact of reality leads to seven ways or modes of description. These are combinations of affirmation and negation:

1. Existence,
2. Non-existence,
3. Occurrence (successive) of Existence and Non-existence,
4. Inexpressibility or Indeterminateness,
5. Inexpressibility as qualified by Existence,
6. Inexpressibility as qualified by Non-existence, and
7. Inexpressibility as qualified by both Existence and Non-existence.

The fourth mode of inexpressibility or *avayakta* is the key element of the Syadvada dialectic. This is especially well brought out by our discussion of wave-particle duality in modern physics. (See also P.C. Mahalanobis, and J.B.S. Haldane,

Sankhya, May 1957, Indian Statistical Institute, Calcutta. Their papers deal with the significance of Syadvada for the foundations of modern statistics.)

Take any meaningful statement. Call it 'A'. It may describe a fact of experience. It could be proposition of logic or mathematics. The Syadvada dialectic demands that in the very nature of things the negative of the given statement is also correct. Denote by Not-A the negative statement of 'A'. The conditions under which the two statements, A and Not-A, are correct cannot, of course, be the same. In general the respective conditions are mutually exclusive. Given a statement 'A', it may not be at all easy to discover the conditions or situations under which Not-A holds. It may even appear at the time impossible. But faith in Syadvada should keep us on to continue the search. For example, in the geometry of Euclid, the sum of the three angles of a triangle is two right angles. The negation of this theorem is a new geometry in which the sum of three angles of a triangle is not equal to two right angles. It was some two thousand years after Euclid that non-Euclidean geometry was discovered in the nineteenth century. Einstein's theory of general relativity is based on this geometry.

Let us consider another idealised situation, which brings out the essentials. Suppose there is an 'atom' in a closed 'box'. The box is divided by a partition into two equal compartments. The partition has a very small hole so that the atom can pass through it (Fig. 4). The hole can be closed if desired. According to classical logic the atom can be either in the left compartment (L) or in the right compartment (R). There is no third alternative. But the new physics forces us to admit other possibilities to explain adequately the results of experiments.

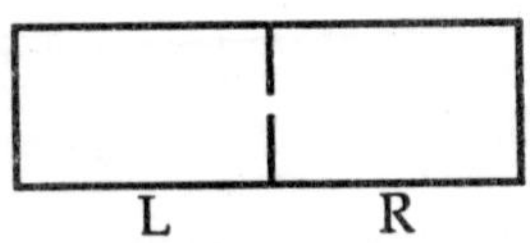

Fig. 4

If we at all use the word 'box' and 'atom', then there is

no escape whatsoever from admitting — in some strange way which totally defies description in words — *that the same atom is, at the same time, in both the compartments*. What we are speaking of is not a case of the atom being sometimes in the left compartment and some times in the right compartment; but being in *both* the compartments at the same time. It is an idea crazy beyond words. And so it is. But there is no escape.

In an earlier section we saw that all electrons in the universe form a single brotherhood, they are all truly identical. There is absolutely no way that we can identify two electrons, or for that matter two atoms (isotopes) of the same element, as different. Recently NASA (USA) scientists have built atomic clock to measure time with an accuracy of about 1 minute in 100 billion years, the approximate age of the universe. They utilise the fact that quantum mechanically every atom in the clock is identical with every other one.

The concept of identity of all human beings has also been advocated by many great thinkers and saints. For example, Buddha says: "Learning is a good thing; but it availeth not. True wisdom can be acquired by practice only. Practice the truth that thy brother is the same as thou. Walk in the noble path of righteousness and thou wilt understand that while there is death in self, there is immortality in truth". His teachings on the concept of identity and non-identity are given in greater detail in the second Part of the Book. The great physicist Erwin Schrodinger, who had also studied eastern philosophy in great depth, arrived at similar conclusions. In his book "My View of the World" he writes:

"What is it that has called you so suddenly out of nothingness to enjoy for a brief while a spectacle which remains indifferent to you? The conditions for your existence are almost as old as the rocks. For thousands of years men have striven and suffered and begotten and women have brought forth in pain. A hundred years ago, perhaps, another man sat on this spot; like you he gazed with awe and yearning in his heart at the dying light on the glaciers. Like you he was begotten of man and born of woman. He felt pain and brief joy as you do.

Was he someone else? Was it not you yourself? What is this Self of yours? ... What justifies you in obstinately discovering this difference — the difference between you and someone else — when objectively what is there is *the same*? "(For details see Part II of this Book).

Science and religion thus represent two great systems of human thought. In India there has never been a big divide between these and the west has also gradually come round to realise this. Einstein said: " Everyone who is seriously involved in the pursuit of science becomes convinced that a spirit is manifest in the laws of the Universe, a spirit vastly superior to that of man, and one in the face of which we with our modest powers must feel humble. In this way, the pursuit of science leads to a religious feeling of a special sort, which is indeed quite different from the religiosity of someone more naive."

Neils Bohr strongly advocated and hoped that one day the complementarity principle would be a part of school and general education for everyone.

V. Education and Character Building

Our modern world is characterised by an extremely rapid pace of change. In some essential ways the shape of the world changes beyond recognition within the lifetime of a generation. Such a rapid rate of change is a new thing in man's history. So rapid is the growth of knowledge that a young man receiving a master's degree in a modern subject is nearly obsolescent on the day of his graduation. A degree, like a passport, would need to be revalidated every five or ten years. A research paper, if a good one, is often out-of-date on the day of its publication. An expensive research tool is out of fashion by the time it is procured.

Such rapid changes tend to increase tensions among people leading to anti-social behaviour, delinquency and criminality. The job of facing these dangers and preparing the people to adopt to the rapidly changing environment, which is a characteristic of our times, falls on education. It is only education which can prepare people to face the future.

A sound education for all is therefore an essential requirement for the progress of any country — particularly a developing one. The best and most profitable investment a country can make is in the education of its children. Top priority should go to free primary education of at least 4 to 5 years duration for all children. It should be effective education, otherwise it would be waste of resources and even worse. This requires sustained and careful research in how primary education is to be organised and supported (see Appendix).

Unfortunately, in India the number of illiterates in the population has been increasing gradually over the years. Although good intentions have a long ancestry in our country, they are hardly ever transformed into action. The Indian Constitution envisaged a fully literate India in ten years, whereas the 1964 Education Commission urged that by 1986 illiteracy should be almost completely eradicated as a step vital to industrialisation and development of agriculture. Gandhi wrote: "character building has the first place in it and that is primary education. A building created on this foundation will last."

We in India are basically still being governed by laws framed by the Britishers when they ruled the country. It is therefore not at all surprising that our educational system continues to be the same as we had during the colonial times. It is interesting to recall a report on 'Review on Education' brought out by the Government of India, almost a century back (around 1905):

"The defects of educational system in India are well known and need not be re-stated. They have been largely due to want of funds. Of late years there has been real progress in removing them. In the last decade the total expenditure from all sources on education has risen from 4 crores to nearly 7½ crores.

"Secondary education of one grade or another is the basis of all professional or industrial training in India. The inferior output of secondary schools invades colleges and technical institutions and hinders the development of higher education. At the Allahabad conference the directors of public instruction unanimously regarded the reform of secondary English schools as the most urgent of educational problems.

"The Government of India have for some time had under consideration the improvement of the pay and prospects of the educational services, Indian, provincial and subordinate... The Government of India recognise that improvement in the position of all the educational services is required, so as to attract first class men in increasing numbers, and while leaving questions of reorganisation for the consideration of the commission, are considering minor proposals for the improvement of the position of these services. They attach the greatest importance to provision for the old age of teachers, either by pension or provident fund. It is not possible to have a healthy moral atmosphere in any school, primary or secondary or at any college when the teacher is discontented and anxious about the future.

"The propositions that illiteracy must be broken down and that primary education has, in the present circumstances of India, a predominant claim upon the public funds, represent accepted policy no longer open to discussion. For financial and administrative reasons of decisive weight the Government of India have refused to recognise the principle of compulsory education; but they desire the widest possible extension of primary education on a voluntary basis."

Let us consider the case of Russia after the Communist Revolution in October 1917. During the very first years after the revolution 'everybody who could read and write joined in a sweeping campaign to eliminate illiteracy. [Around 72 per cent of the population (83 per cent of women) were illiterate at the time.] People went to classes after their workday. Instruction in reading and writing was given everywhere — in schools, workers' clubs, factories, workers' settlements and villages, big and small. It was a real nationwide crusade against illiteracy.'*

In 1971, Leonid Brezhnev said: "The society we are building presupposes high educational standards of the people as a whole and a rich cultural life. In the current five-year plan

* Alexei Kolinin, The Soviet System of Public Education. Novosti Press. Moscow 1973.

period the transition to universal secondary education (ages 17 to 18 years) is to be completed throughout the country."

Gandhiji strongly advocated that all children should be trained in handicrafts, apart from receiving formal education in schools. In India, unfortunately, hardly any attention has been paid to this aspect of education. In the Soviet Union great emphasis was given to handicrafts and practical training. Handicraft lessons were started for classes 1 to 3 and practical training was provided to students of 4th class onwards. Practical work occupied almost 140 hours in a year. Vocational training was also started for students and necessary facilities were provided in schools attached to factories, enterprises, farms, etc.

It is interesting to recall that industrial progress in Europe started after compulsory school education for all children was introduced, and not the other way round. For any underdeveloped country to progress, it is almost imperative that it pays full attention to sound education of all its citizens.

The Education Commission Report of 1964-66 begins:

'The destiny of India is now being shaped in her classrooms. This, we believe, is no mere rhetoric. In a world based on science and technology, it is education that determines the level of prosperity, welfare and security of the people. On the quality and number of persons coming out of our schools and colleges will depend our success in the great enterprise of national reconstruction the principal objective of which is to raise the standard of living of our people'. Even the former U.S. President, Thomas Jefferson remarked: 'If a nation expects to be ignorant and free, it expects what never was and never will be'. In his book *'Basic Education'*, Gandhi quotes Professor Huxley: '...who has learnt to hate all vileness and to respect others as himself. Such a one and no other, I conceive, has had a liberal education, for he is in harmony with nature. He will make the best of her and she of him.' According to a German saying 'Education is what remains after what you learnt in school is forgotten'.

To provide a strong foundation for a peaceful world we need a sound educational system. We must try and inculcate in our children from very young age, love and admiration for nature. They must learn to appreciate what marvellous thing life is. Primary education needs utmost attention. It has been emphasised by almost all great thinkers. Gandhi wrote: 'I am a firm believer in the principle of free and compulsory Primary Education for India. I also hold that we shall realise this only by teaching the children a useful vocation and utilising it as a means for cultivating their mental, physical and spiritual faculties'. He further wrote: 'We have upto now concentrated on stuffing children's minds with all kinds of information, without ever thinking of stimulating and developing them. Let us now cry a halt and concentrate on educating the child properly through manual work, not as a side activity, but as a prime means of intellectual training'. In a different language, similar thoughts have been expressed by John W. Gardner, former President of Carnegie Corporation, New York (USA): 'The child is a model of openness to experience — receptive, curious, eager, unafraid, willing to try anything. As the years pass these priceless qualities fade. He becomes more cautious, less eager and accumulates deeply rooted habits and fixed attitudes. ... We are stuffing their heads with the products of earlier innovations rather then teaching them how to innovate. We think of the mind as a store house to be filled, rather than as an instrument to be used'.

Popularisation of science is essential for the health and progress of the nation. And the difficulty is not that science is inherently difficult to communicate. In fact, basically, science is easy to communicate. The real trouble is lack of earnest and sustained effort to make science accessible to the common man. To learn science is to do science: and one can do a lot of interesting science, both physical and biological, with readily available materials and appliances in homes and farms. Also, every school and college can make a very significant contribution to popularise science. At the dawn of Indian Independence, speaking at the 1947 session of the Indian Science Congress, Pandit Jawaharlal Nehru declared that science "must think in terms of the few hundred million persons in India."

To promote science education and dissemination of science, Professor Kothari started in 1971, the National Science Exhibition for Children. The first exhibition was inaugurated on November 14, 1971 — the birthday of Pandit Nehru, by the then President of India, Shri V.V. Giri. While speaking at the inauguration Dr. Kothari said:

"The purpose of the Science Exhibition is to promote science education and dissemination of science. A visit to the Exhibition gives us a "feel" of the excitement and creativity of science and technology. It helps to appreciate the great power and complexity of science, as also the deeply inspiring grandeur and beauty of scientific abstractions. Many examples of "Mathematical beauty" immediately come to mind. A classic case is the discovery, based on the work of Professor S.N. Bose, that all particles in nature can be classified in terms of the symmetry of their wave functions: Particles are either bosons (named after BOSE) or fermions (named after FERMI).

"An exhibition provides an occasion for co-operative effort and an opportunity to learn from one another's experience, students and teachers together. It reinforces initiative, innovation and creativity. A major aim of this Exhibition is to encourage a wide use for science education of easily available materials and local resources. The immense potentialities of adapting simple inexpensive things, toys and kits (strings and sealing-wax, to use an old phrase) for class experiments, demonstrations and teaching aids is not enough realised. We could learn far more by fully exploiting simple devices, from improvisations, than we would from expensive apparatus poorly used as is often the situation. In the first case one has got to think and do continuing research, whereas in the latter case it is largely a question of spending money — usually someone else's money.

"The modern world is knowledge based, largely science and technology based. Two crucial questions for us and for nearly all countries (including the most advanced in science) are: Firstly, how can science and mathematics education (imparted on a large scale) be made an exciting experience for pupil and teacher relevant, creative and humanistic. The response to this challenge has initiated a revolution in science and mathematics education. The second question is: How science growing at a terrific rate can be 'popularised'. How can science and even more importantly the spirit of science, be communicated to the people without gross distortion and misrepresentation.

"Science exhibitions, if carefully planned and organised, can make a significant contribution to these two themes." He further said: "Science exhibitions provide opportunities for public communication of science... It is now becoming increasingly apparent that the capabilities of young children to grasp abstract mathematical and scientific concepts have been in the past very much, if not grossly, under-rated... The need for a radical change in science education has been felt everywhere for a long time."

"The way science is taught today to most pupils in most countries, it hardly helps to promote curiosity and the spirit of inquiry. In fact, not unoften, it tends to kill questioning, creativity and originality: Science as generally taught kills the spirit of science. We recall the words of Albert Einstein: He says about his life at the Polytechnic Institute of Zurich, which he entered at the age of 17:

"The mass of insufficiently connected experimental data was overwhelming here also. In this field, however, I soon learned to scent out that which was able to lead to fundamentals and to turn aside from everything else, from the multitude of things which clutter up the mind and divert it from the essential. The hitch in this was of course, the fact that one had to cram all this stuff into one's mind for the examinations, whether one liked it or not. This coercion had such a deterring effect (upon me) that, after I had passed the final examination, I found the consideration of any scientific problems distasteful to me for an entire year. In justice I must add, moreover, that in Switzerland we had to suffer far less under such coercion, which smoothers every truly scientific impulse, than is the case in many another locality. There were altogether only two examinations; aside from these, one could just about do as one pleased. This was especially the case if one had a friend, as did

I, who attended the lectures regularly and who worked over their content conscientiously. This gave one freedom in the choice of pursuits until a few months before the examination, a freedom, which I enjoyed to a great extent and have gladly taken into the bargain the bad conscience, connected with it as by far the lesser evil. It is, in fact, nothing short of a miracle that the modern methods of instruction have not yet entirely strangled the holy curiosity of inquiry; for this delicate little plant, aside from stimulation, stands mainly in need of freedom; without this it goes to wreck and ruin without fail. It is a very grave mistake to think that the enjoyment of seeing and searching can be promoted by means of coercion and a sense of duty."

[Albert Einstein: *The Library of Living Philosophers* (1949), p. 17].

The importance of a proper early education has been lucidly and forcefully brought out by the American Educationist, Robert Fulghum, in his best seller: 'All I Really Need to Know I Learned in Kindergarten'. He writes:

'All I really need to know about how to live and what to do and how to be I learned in Kindergarten. Wisdom was not at the top of the graduate school mountain, but there in the sandpile at Sunday school. These are the things I learned:

Share everything.
Play fair.
Don't hit people.
Put things back where you found them.
Clean up your mess.
Don't take things that aren't yours.

When you go out into the world, watch out for traffic, hold hands and stick together.

Be aware of wonder. Remember the little seed in the Styrofoam cup. The roots go down and the plant goes up and nobody really knows how or why, but we all like that.

Goldfish and hamsters and white mice and even seed in the Styrofoam cup — they all die. So do we.

And then remember the Dick-and-Jane books and the first word you learned — the biggest word of all — Look'.

He goes on to add: 'And it is still true, no matter how old you are — when you go out into the world, it is best to hold hands and stick together'.

Let us consider another example from Japan — country unique in many ways. The first chapter of the booklet 'Course of Study of Elementary Schools (I to VI grades) in Japan' brought out by the Ministry of Education, Science and Culture of the Government of Japan, deals with general provisions. The first paragraph, in part, states that 'each school should formulate a proper curriculum in compliance with the provisions of the laws and regulations concerned.....' The second paragraph reads as follows:

'It should be a basic principle that moral education in the school should be provided throughout all the educational activities of the school. Therefore, proper instructions for moral development should be given not only in the hours for Moral Education, but also in the hours for each subject and special activities, in conformity with their respective characteristics. In carrying out moral education at school, due consideration should be given to establishing closer human relationships between teachers and pupils and among pupils themselves, and to guiding thoroughly the practice of moral codes in the basic behaviour of everyday life in co-operation with the home and the local community concerned'. (Similar statements are made in the courses of lower and upper secondary schools as well.)

The following subjects are taught in the elementary school to all students — boys and girls: Japanese Language, Social Studies, Arithmetic, Science, Music, Arts and Handicrafts, Home making, Physical education, Moral education and Social activities. The objectives of the science course in grade I are:

'1. To make pupils recognise conspicuous features of living things in their surroundings through such activities as searching for and taking care of them, and experience the pleasure of intimacy with them.

2. To have pupils familiarise themselves with surrounding natural things and phenomena, recognise conspicuous features of them through observations and experiments, and experience the pleasure of contact with them.'

We thus see that the objective of science course can only be to develop appreciation and love of nature. If this objective can be achieved, even in part, it would go a long way in ensuring a peaceful and non-violent society.

Among the various points mentioned for emphasis in the course on Moral Education, are:

> To hold life in high regard, to promote good health and to maintain safety,
> To respect another's freedom as well as one's own, and to be responsible for one's own acts.
> To love justice and hate injustice, and to act righteously with courage,
> To endure hardships and persist to the end for the accomplishment of one's right aims,
> To love nature, and to have affection towards animals and plants with a tender heart,
> To esteem beautiful and noble things, and to have a pure mind,
> To be kind to everybody, and to take care of the weak and the unfortunate,
> To be fair and impartial to everybody without prejudice,
> To understand others feelings and positions, and to forgive others faults generously,
> To appreciate the value of work and co-operate actively in the service of others,
> To take care of public property and to protect public morality with a full awareness of being a member of society,
> To love the nation with pride as a Japanese and to contribute to the development of the nation,

> To have proper understanding of the love towards the people of the entire world and to become an individual who can contribute to the welfare of mankind.

Similar sentiments were expressed in a letter written by Abraham Lincoln to the Head Master of the school in which his son was studying. He wrote, among other things:

> 'In school teach him that it is far more honourable to fail than to cheat.
> Teach him to have faith in his own ideas, even if everyone tells him they are wrong.
> Try to give him the strength not to follow the crowd when everyone is getting on the bandwagon.
> Teach him to listen to all men, but teach him also to filter all he hears on a screen of truth, and take only the good that comes through.
> Teach him how to laugh when he is sad.
> Teach him there is no shame in tears.
> Teach him to close his ears to a howling mob; and to stand and fight if he thinks he's right.
> Treat him gently, but do not cuddle him, because only the test of fire makes fine steel.
> Let him have the courage to be impatient, let him have the patience to be brave.
> Teach him always to have sublime faith in his creator and faith in himself too, because then he will always have faith in mankind.'

C. Rajagopalachari, while in prison in 1922 recorded in his diary:

> 'Elections and their corruptions, injustice and the power and tyranny of wealth, and inefficiency of administration, will make a hell of life as soon as freedom is given to us. Men will look regretfully back to the old regime of comparative justice, and efficient, peaceful, more or less honest administration.

> 'The only thing gained will be that as a race we will be saved from dishonour and subordination.
>
> 'Hope lies only in universal education by which right conduct, fear of God and love will be developed among the citizens from childhood.
>
> 'It is only if we succeed in this that Swaraj will mean happiness. Otherwise it will mean the grinding injustices and tyranny of wealth.....'

It has all come to pass. If the country has to come out of the trap it is presently caught in, it will have to heed much more seriously the teachings of Gandhiji. One may know many things but until one learns to practice them in life, they are of no value. It is here that sound education plays a vital role in realising what is truth and then learning to practice it.

In India, for our educational system to be effective, lot of research still needs to be done on educating our children. What are the questions that arise in the minds of children of a given age, how they change with age; how are these questions related to the geographical and social surroundings; what is the most effective way of educating children of a given age, particularly when children with varied talents and interests are combined in a single class; what role do activities play in the learning process of children; how does the medium of instruction, if it is different from the mother tongue, affect the learning process; etc.?

Large population is considered as a great handicap for the progress of our country. This is only because a very large section of our population continues to be illiterate. It would be a great asset if it were properly educated. It is extremely important that we identify talent and properly nurture it.

Ramanujam could not pass his Intermediate examination (now called Senior Secondary or XII), his sole interest was in mathematics. His talent was identified by Prof. G.H. Hardy of Cambridge University, England, who then arranged to get him there and nurtured him. Though Ramanujam died at an early age of 32 years, he is regarded as one of the most outstanding mathematicians of the last century.

Primary education for every child is most essential for any country. Unfortunately, inspite of more than five decades of independence, we have not yet been able to establish a sound educational system.

Learning science or ethics is something students do and not something that is done to them. As Professor Frank Press, Former President of the National Academy of Sciences, U.S.A., said: 'We must begin early by providing children with a challenging and stimulating introduction to science in the elementary grades — a hands-on experience that will give them a taste of real science and build an appetite for more.'

To promote Truth, which is essential both for science as well as religion, we urgently need a sound educational system. The best investment the country can make is in education.

REFERENCES

Ahmed, Feroz (Editor): *'Education and Character Building, Collection of Convocation Addresses, delivered by Prof. D.S. Kothari,* NISCOM, New Delhi, 2000.

Ahmed, Feroz (Editor): Atom and Self, Collection of Lectures delivered by D.S. Kothari, New Age International Pub., New Delhi, 2002.

Ahmed, Feroz (Editor): *Knowledge and Wisdom, Collection of Lectures and Addresses delivered by D.S. Kothari,* New Age International Pub., New Delhi, 2003.

Carus, Paul: *Gospel of Buddha,* Publication Division, G. of I., Delhi, 1990.

Fulghum, Robert: *All I Really need to Know I Learned in Kindergarten,* Ivy Books, New York, 1988.

Gangrade, K.D.: 'Gandhian Perspective on Education, in *Education for a Global Society,* edited by Mukhopadhyay and Marmer, Shipra Publications', Delhi, 2003: pp. 40-52.

Hardy, G.H.: A Mathematician's Apology, Cambridge University Press, 1948.

Kalinin, Alexei: *The Soviet System of Public Education',* Novosti Press, Moscow, 1973.

Kothari, L.S.: *Education and Peace,* Gandhi Smriti and Darshan Samiti, New Delhi, 2001.

Schrodinger, E.: *What is Life?* Cambridge University Press, Cambridge, 1949.

Schrodinger, E.: *My View of the World,* Cambridge University Press, Cambridge, 1964.

Sherrington, Sir Charles: *Man on His Nature*, Cambridge University Press, Cambridge, 1951.
Ministry of Education, Government of Japan: *Course of Study for Elementary Schools in Japan*, 1983.
Indian National Science Academy: *Selections from and on Einstein*, 1984.

APPENDIX

Urgent Need for Change in Science Curriculum

The advancement of any country in the modern age is totally dependent on the level of science and technology there. Most unfortunately, over the last decades the level of science in India has been gradually declining. To reverse the trend will require great effort and the most important step in this direction will be to completely change the science curriculum and the method of teaching.

We teach science for passing examinations and clearing competition tests. It is taught more like history – emphasis being on early discoveries and innovations. 'The spirit of science' is totally missing from the course – whether it is at school level or collage level. To improve the level of science, teaching of science will have to be totally modified.

1. Science should be taught in the mother tongue of the child. The emphasis should be on understanding the concepts rather than learning by rot.
2. Science is based on truth and cooperation. If taught properly the course can greatly help in inculcating these vital moral values.
3. Teaching of science must be inquiry centred. Students must learn to observe phenomena, design experiments, collect data and discuss their ideas. 'Science' can only be learnt by doing science.

In learning science it is more important to know about what is not known, rather than what is known. Students must be encouraged to ask questions and effort should be made to sustain their curiosity about nature.

4. Learning by doing, or hands-on experience is the only way of learning science. Experiments must find a prominent place in science education, but must be open-ended and not the same year after year.
5. The course covered should not be too heavy or too broad. The emphasis must be on depth. Students must have ample free time available to them to be able to assimilate what they learn and raise questions.
6. The scope of physics and chemistry (and also mathematics) is universal, while in subjects like botany and zoology, the examples one chooses are region dependent. It is therefore important that text-books in these subjects should be different for different regions. For example plant and animal life in Assam is very different from that in Rajasthan or Jammu and Kashmere.
7. One of the most significant contributions of science to human thought is the principle of complementarity discovered by Niels Bohr. It should be taught in schools.
8. Lot of research needs to be done on how our children in different age groups and different social backgrounds learn. Only after we know this can we educate them properly.
9. The entire educational system should be guided by devoted educationists and should enjoy autonomy. It must be free to decide (i) what to teach, (ii) whom to teach and (iii) who will teach.
10. Unfortunately, we have separated research and teaching—collages and universities mainly do the teaching and research institutions carry on research. This has led to the decline of both. Universities must be fully supported to carry out research and persons with commitment to research and teaching should be selected as teachers.

3

Truth and Religion

Swami Vivekananda explained to the "Sisters and Brothers of America" (September 11, 1893) and to the people of the world at large the seminal idea of the fundamental unity of all religions, and offered the key to interfaith understanding. He condemned sectarianism and bigotry, and sounded death knell of all forms of fanaticism and religious persecutions. The time for fulfilling Swami Vivekananda's clarion call has come, and therefore, we should make an exemplary beginning (Singhvi, 2002) in our country for its realisation.

The Vedic world-view fostered tolerance by declaring: "The Truth is one; there are different pathways to it" [Ekam Sat Viprah Bahudha Vadanti]. The Sarmana Jain tradition also declared that the Truth exists [Sachham Lokamni Saarbohooyam] in all its diversities. It fostered tolerance on the basis of the doctrine of Anekanwad, which is based on the theory of many aspects of truth and many routes to truth in the dialectic of opposites (Singhvi, HT, Sep. 11, 2002, p 12).

The spirit of Vendanta and Anekandta as well as the teachings of saints and seers facilitated thoughtful dialogues, which became a way of life in India. It is not as if there were never any feuds between the people of different persuasions in ancient India, but were comparatively fewer in numbers and also less violent.

Civilisations have had a trial and pugnacious streak in them and have often been less than civil in their encounters with each other. Although they were marked by creative cross-fertilisation, they looked at each other as aliens with bloodshot eyes. It is in this context that we ought to recall the exceptional 'civil' message of the age old Indian axiom of Vasudhaiva Kutumbakam (the world is one family) and its underlying thought process, which rejects the mindset of the otherness of the other as trivial prejudice and removes narrow-mindedness of the people. The Vedic exhortation is to look upon everyone with friendly eyes [mitrasya cakoura sameekshamahe] (Singhvi, HT, Sep. 11, 2002, p. 12).

The Jains and Buddhists insisted on adherence to the tenets of universal friendship, forgiveness, non-violence, compassion, and their relevance for life. Conflicts between kingdoms and religious establishments did occur frequently, but at the level of thought, there was a great deal of freedom, tolerance and civility. Protests and disputations, both articulated and many but clash of arms and use of force in the name and for the cause of religions were rare (Singhvi, HT, Sep. 11, 2002).

There are few Anniversaries as black as the one that we recalled recently on September 11. It was the first anniversary of the terrorist attacks on certain US targets by Islamic fundamentalists on September 11, 2001. Only the Hiroshima Day, which falls on August 6, is remembered as an event more ghastly than the terrorist attacks on US. It may not be out of place to mention here that the first atom bomb was dropped over Hiroshima on 6th of August 1945. However, the significance of Hiroshima Day lies in telling the world about the horrors of a nuclear war. But the only meaning, which September 11 carries, is that of the naked terrorism. The Hiroshima ended a war. But the perpetrators of the September 11 massacre wanted to begin one. The more frightening aspect is that the terrorists, inspired by a perverted fascination with the medieval concept of holy war against infidel, represent nihilism of such a kind that has been rarely seem before (HT Editorial, September 11, 2002).

While remembering the massacres of 2001, it is necessary for every country to rededicate itself to the cause of 'freedom' so that no one will be scared of boarding a plane or go to office or the market or the children's playground. India has lived with the terrorism long enough to know that only an untrammelled expression of the "popular will" is the best antidote to terror.

Unfortunately, the countries, which are the breeding grounds of disaffection — Afghanistan, Pakistan, Saudi Arabia and other Islamic countries — are virtually under dictatorships. As long as they remain so, it will not be easy to eliminate Jehadis...it is the spirit of freedom, which is bound to triumph over terror (HT Editorial, Sep. 11, 2002).

The centennial World's Parliament of Religions held in 1993 transcreated the legacy of Vivekananda through a declaration titled "Towards a Global Ethic". Between 1893 and 1993, the world has witnessed two great wars, the tragic Holocaust, rise of racism, religious fanaticism and terrorism. Here, we need to remember Gandhi who said that the various religions are like leaves of a tree which might seem different, but are, in fact one (Singhvi, ToI, Sep. 11, 2002).

The 1993 Parliament emphasised the moral and spiritual roots of human civilisation. It took a leaf from Vivekananda's teachings regarding concerns for the human conditions. The declaration condemned the social disarray of nations, overtaking our communities and aggression and hatred in the name of religion. It affirmed that there already existed a basis for a global ethics to lead humanity to better tomorrow (Singhvi, ToI, Sep. 11, 2002).

Tolerance is the golden thread that runs through the Universal Declaration. It is the safest foundation for a decent civil society. Indeed, the fundamental duty of tolerance is woven into every form and fabric of secularism, freedom and democracy and the rules of law. We need the fundamentalism of tolerance and togetherness for the success of a decent civil society every where in the world. Here and now, the place and time for the "Talisman" of tolerance to build a happier and harmonious future for humanity (Singhvi, ToI, Sep. 11, 2002).

It is a common proposition that claims of absolute truth leading to confrontation, while a belief in relativity of truth is in a favourable dialogue. Is truth relative? Some people say: What I believe is true for me and what you believe is true for you, that truth is relative to the person. Is it so? Before one proceeds further, two clarifications will be helpful; (i) to claim that truth is relative could mean either that (a) truth itself is relative which is a metaphysical statement, or (b) that it can only be known relatively is an epistemological statement. The latter view leaves room for the existence of an absolute truth metaphysically, the former does not. (ii) Similarly, to claim that truth is relative could imply (a) the denial of an extra-personal reality altogether, or (b) imply that though such an extra personal truth exist, it can be known only by a person and is therefore relative to the person. To say that truth is relative could mean that as the outside world is known to us through the mind which is assisted in its operations by the senses, "we cannot talk of the existence of external objects without reference to any mind." And, as such, a mind has to be that of a "person", the knowledge of the object must relate to the person and is therefore relational and therefore relative to the person relating to it. Truth is, therefore relative (Sharma, 2002).

To say that truth is relative could also mean that even if the external reality of objects is conceded, their perception of each individual is unique to him and not identical with that of other person. Hence, when ten people look at a vase, for instance, none looks at it exactly from the same angle or sees exactly the same surface. In this sense truth could be relative even in a system of objective realism. Even on this view, however, one must admit "that" although there may be slightly differing perceptions of "what" it is.

Even if the vase exists by itself independently of how it is perceived, there may be a further sense in which it could be said that the truth about it is relative. For, all that we can claim on perceiving the vase is that our correct cognition of it corresponds to the object, but how do we know that the cognition corresponds to the "reality" or the object. A person looking at a vase with a microscope will see a different object, with a telescope another, and with the naked eye yet another. Does the reality of the object consist of all these "visions"? What if these views of the vase are multiplied with instruments of variable caliber? Which view would represent the object? It therefore becomes relative to the instrument and the person using the instrument or alternatively an endless collage of all these multiplying "views".

Several propositions can be assumed in relation to the relativity of truth: Skepticism, Relativism, Absolutism, and Agnosticism. Let these be understood as follows:

- Skepticism implies that both the knowledge of religion and reality are indeterminate.
- Relativism implies that the knowledge of reality may be relative but not necessarily the reality itself.
- Absolutism usually implies that both the knowledge and the object of knowledge are determinate.
- Agnosticism usually implies that we cannot be certain of any of the above positions.

These positions now may be brought in relation to dialogue. If the statement "truth is relative" is understood sceptically, then inter-religious dialogue is in fact a religious dialogue, say among non-believing academics. If the statement is understood relativistically, then inter-religious dialogues possess the kind of flavour associated with the Indian religious tradition.

If the statement is understood absolutically, then inter-religious dialogues possess the kind of flavour associated with religious tradition. If the statement is understood agnostically, then either there is no dialogue or it is at best humorous and at worst frivolous (Sharma, 2002, p. 98).

Spiritual or truthful living is responsible living. Gandhi said: "I am responsible not for myself but for all of you just as all of you are responsible for me. When we live truly selfless life we never think in terms of personal or pleasure but always in terms of global prosperity and world peace. For even these grand goals ultimately depend not on governments but on selfless effort of little people like you and me." In the long run, friendly persuasion is the only effective way of teaching. Human beings are educable, human beings can always grow. "If the man gains spiritually", Gandhi said, "The whole world gains with him."

The ancient Hindu scriptures wonderfully say, "May all creatures be happy. May people every where live in abiding peace and love. For all of us are one, and joy can be found only in the joy of all."

In life, religion helps us to go from one stage of life to another smoothly. When threatened by cruel circumstances and crises, it helps creating such strongness in one's personality that enables one to sustain oneself against vicissitudes of life. As soon as religious values and hopes for a better life vanish from a person's experiences, they stop living and begin to die. If we destroy "hope", we destroy "future".

Hope strengthens our will to survive calamities, and therefore, a person who hopes, never gives way to despair. Educating the people is the only way to achieve our cherished goal of peace. There are four main institutions that can sustain the value system namely, the family, education, political and religious institutions. The fact is that in the present situation none of these four are in a good condition. Consequently, the value system has come to a state of great degeneration. These institutions need to be strengthened to inculcate right values in coming generations.

The bad effect of electronic and print media also needs to be controlled. Admittedly, a philosopher such as Rousseau and an activist like Alexander Kernsky held that "those people like Machiavelli who treat politics and morality separately, will never understand either of the things." In India, Gandhi and his first mentor, G.K. Gokhale seriously discussed the techniques by which spiritualism and religious morality could be introduced into Indian politics. But after almost more than half a century of Swaraj, despite code of conduct and ethical injunctions, politics is far removed for any moral tenet. The official motto, "truth will prevail" faces huge hurdles in practice.

Gandhi was a synthesiser. There are so many demerits in modern civilisation that he rejects, but not the liberal contributions of modernity, civil liberties, equality, alleviation of poverty, religious tolerance etc. Rather his effort can be interpreted as an attempt to integrate these positive elements with a liberal interpretation of tradition. Even some see him as radical and others as reactionary. Gandhi is popularly perceived as a great synthesiser of countries, if not of contradictions, within and across traditions.

His Purna Swaraj would harmonise rights and duties, head and heart, individual and community, faith and reason, economic development and spiritual progress, religious commitment and religious pluralism, self-realisation and political action. Blind faith of fundamentalist, revivalist version of religion was totally unacceptable to Gandhi. He would instantly question faith to ascertain whether it was meaningful and reasonable in terms of basic human values, and he would demand of reason the same fidelity to these values as well. He urges us the injunction of the Isopanishad: Enjoy the things of the earth by renouncing them. We do not have to idealise Gandhi into a new "ism". We need the open-ended critique of Gandhi, not a close-ended "ism". Gandhi is, indeed, greater than "Gandhi-ism."

For Gandhi, truth was God (Truth = God). Let us give some extracts from the text of the speech delivered by Gandhi in September 1931 during his visit to the Round Table Conference:

> "There is an indefinable mysterious power that pervades everything, I feel it through. I do not see it. It transcends the senses. But it is possible to reason out the existence of God to a limited extent. Even in ordinary affairs we know that people do not know who rules or why and how they rule and yet they know that there is power that certainly rules. In my tour last year in Mysore (Karnataka) I met many poor villagers and It is found upon inquiry that they did not know who ruled Mysore. They simply said some God ruled it. If the knowledge of these poor people is limited about their ruler, I, who am infinitely lesser in respect to God than they to their ruler, need not be surprised, if I do not realise the presence of God — the king of Kings. Nevertheless, I do feel as the poor villagers, felt about Mysore that there is orderliness in the universe, there is an unalterable law governing everything and every being that exists or lives. It is not a blind law, for no blind law can govern

> the conduct of living beings and thanks to the marvellous research of Sri J.C. Bose, it can now be proved that even matter has life. That law which governs all life is God. God to be God must rule the heart and transform it. *Exercise of faith will be the safest course to believe in the moral government of world and therefore there is the supremacy of the moral law and the law of truth and love, two pillars of peace* (emphasis added)."

Khushwant Singh, while commenting on the Encyclopaedia of God, says: "From the time life began on earth people have been asking themselves who or what made us; what was his/her or its purpose, where do we go, when do we die...all we have is an assertion about a God, who one fine day decided to create life, gave different creatures different names, different spans of life and then made them disappear forever. Sometime people thought there must be hundred of thousands of creators who looked after different aspects of life. Others argued there should be one creator. They called it God. Still later came philosopher and prophets. In West Asia we had Zoroaster, Abraham and Moses, Jesus Christ and Mohammed. Their followers founded themselves into separate groups and sought to impose their views on others. In India we have Mahavir and Gautam Buddha. Both of them did not accept the existence of God, but laid down norms of social behaviour and acquired large followers. Their predominance was challenged by Adi Shankara who was able to re-establish Hindu predominance."

There were serious challenges to the caste classified Hindu Society. These challenges were met in battlefields as well as in attempts to an understanding between each other. From the Hindu side, they were the Bhaktas, notably Kabir and Nanak; from the Muslim side, Sufis, notably Farid, Meunuddin and Nizamuddin of the Chistia order. The process of coming to an understanding between contending faiths continued.

The relevance of Gandhi seems to grow and not diminish because his abiding faith in the innate goodness of man and oneness of all religions. Religion to be religion must rule the heart and transform mankind to achieve world peace. Gandhi popularised soul force, which is but another name for love force, in place of brute force.

Politicians in general, instead of giving moral leadership, for which people are yearning and wailing, are only occupied in maintaining a system, which is poisoned by collective bad faith and polluted by individual self-interest. The two basic lessons, which we are to learn from Indian history and from Gita are:

1. People have always taken their moral standards from their rulers and have risen to great heights. Whenever they have followed in the glow of noble kings or leaders; and
2. Regions and Kingdoms have been destroyed not by adversies but by abasement and corruption.

We need world leaders who would lead us and believe in the eternal values of faith, compassion and respect for all. This will win the day and make us worthy inheritors of the Gandhian legacy.

To create a culture of peace we need, "globalisation from below" with a solid recognition that this globalisation is only possible with the active participation of men and women from all countries. Peace is not created *de novo* out of diplomatic activity. It is created out of the every day skills of peaceful problem-solving and conflict resolution in families, neighbourhoods and among different social, cultural, religious and ethnic groups within and between societies.

In order to achieve eternal peace in the world we must all avoid seven sins identified by Gandhi. These are:

1. Politics without principle
2. Pleasure without conscience
3. Commerce without ethics (morality)
4. Knowledge without character
5. Science without humanity
6. Wealth without work
7. Worship without sacrifice

(*Young India*, 22nd October, 1925)

The Mahatma dealt with the problems, which are timeless and universal, because they spring from enduring weakness of human nature and human society. Since the solutions to be found for them were based on eternal varieties, his influence and his relevance are also timeless and universal.

In the ultimate analysis "Self Realisation" is the only way to achieve peace, for in its absence there will be neither true religion nor peace. It needs to be constantly nurtured. The electronic media (especially T.V.) is playing havoc with our value system. In India, an average eight-year-old Indian child has seen more than 1,000 murders and 500 rape scenes on media. This is true as well in other parts of the world. In an advertisement the message may be more subtle but leaves a deeper impression.

The Golden rule to be adopted by all of us is: "Treat others as you would have them treat you." Inner violence is capable of creating havoc on the lives of others. Plato said: "May I do unto others as I would have others do unto me." The wisdom of Confucius, Jain tenets, Christian teachings, Islam, Sikhism and many other religions and schools of thought voice the same maxim.

Genuine concern for the Global Peace necessarily leads to awareness of inter-dependent communities as Gandhi envisaged. It includes not only human kind but it extends to the transcending geographic, cosmic and temporal boundaries across generations.

The latest craze that has caught the eye of the corporate sector is SQ. Spiritual Quotient is the most important attribute of a human being and the foundation of both IQ (Intelligent Quotient) and EQ (Emotional Quotient). Some studies have found that a spiritual awakening among staff members had led to remarkable growth on the productivity of the company.

I shall like to echo Gandhi's words that we should all make it a point in promoting inter-faith dialogue and understanding. The aforesaid analysis has led me to conclude that the essential unity of all religions has been universality of LOVE as the binding principle of all faiths. It is cardinally implied that there is no place of HATRED between people professing different faiths.

Gandhi hoped that 'the individual being pure, sacrifices himself for the family, the latter for the village, the village for the district, the district for the province, the province for the nation, the nation for all. (Young India, 28th May, 1931)

Gandhi was a "practical idealist", as one who combined high moral adventure with a series of "experiment with truth." In 1936 he observed: "The opinion I have formed and the conclusions I have arrived are not final, I may change them tomorrow. I have nothing new to teach the world. Truth and non-violence are as old as the hills. All I have done is to try experiments on both on as vast scale as possible." To him, his experiment with Truth was even more important than his experiment with non-violence. Thus, he said "As a Jain Muni once rightly said, I was not so much votary of *ahimsa* as I was of truth..." I was capable of sacrificing non-violence for the sake of truth". It was this pursuit of rational truth, which imparted to his social philosophy a quality of fascinating coherence. He was not an activist without a systematic social philosophy. It was a coherent social philosophy that gave him self-assurance not only as a vivacious controversialist, but also as a man of action who had to take decisions on moments of crisis. (Ganguli, 1973)

In 1947, when Gandhi's feeble voice was in the wilderness, which many people did not wish to hear but which still refused to be silenced, he spoke of with the calm self-assurance of a person to whom his social philosophy had revealed its unity of design just as controversial work of art reveals the beauty of the composition to a painter. He said, "Some suggest that I should not speak at all. This multitude of advisers remind me of a painter who had exposed his painting in a shop window without glass, inviting the critics of mark the parts they did not like. The result was a daub. The painter had simply tried to show that it was impossible to please all parties. His business was to produce a work, which satisfied his artistic taste. Mine (Gandhiji) is a similar case". (Ganguli, 1973, p. 11)

Is Gandhi's social philosophy itself not an ideology in the sense in which one understands warring ideologies? Since non-violence is its essence, can one not say that it is not an ideology that depends upon violence for its validity and survival? Marx feared Marxism as much as Gandhism. Both of them distrusted dogmatism and doctrine. As early as 1924, Romain Rolland — an admirer of both Gandhi and Lenin — tried to explore the possibility of approachment between the two. In Europe, Gandhi's social thought had been infused with pacifism. Romain Rolland said: I wished to see in the fighting communism of USSR and the Civil Disobedience of India, organised by Gandhi, the two great wings of the revolution. Romain Rolland anticipated that "a project of that sort was bound to break against the intransigence of the two faiths, each of which considered itself to be in sole possession of the truth: the truth of the other seemed to be an enemy". Did Gandhi's movement and Lenin's revolution then stand in relation to each other as warring ideologies? Romain Rolland was unsure of his position, because he saw in the most powerful or religious doctrines not dogmas, but vigorous hypotheses laying down a road for the advancement of men. Gandhi however told him that his socio-political movement was all "experiment" — an experiment is not known. Nevertheless, Romain Rolland went on to speak of "two experiments, the two greatest the two most efficacious, the only one efficacious enough to reach the world of men away from the catastrophe into which it is about to plunge". He thought that the two together would not be more than adequate to secure its salvation. Romain Rolland wanted movements to converge and unite to fight a common enemy. Gandhi believed in the co-existence of opposing ideologies and their eventual synthesis though peaceful competition and interaction among them. Gandhi said, "All that I know of Bolshevism is that it aims at the abolition of the institution of private property. This is an application of the ethical ideal of non-possession in the realm of economics. If the people adopted ideal of their own accord or could be made to accept it by means of peaceful persuasion there could be nothing like it. But from what I know of Bolshevism it not only preclude the use of force but freely sanctions it for the expropriation of private property and maintaining the collective ownership of the same. It is my firm conviction that nothing enduring can be built on violence." (Ganguli, 1973, pp. 356-57)

Helena Petrovna Blavatsky is popularly known and remembered as Madame Blavatsky. She, 127 years ago, founded the Theosophical society in New York. Its objects were to form a nucleus of universal brotherhood of humanity, without distinction of race, creed, sex, caste or colour, study of religions, philosophies and sciences, and investigation of unexplained laws of nature. She brought theosophy to the world in human history — at a time when superstition and materialism had begun to overshadow any quest for truth. Her teachings are embodied in the three major works: *The Secret Doctrine, Isis,* and *the Key to Theosophy*. With ancient and modern science and theosophy, Blavatsky provides a rationale for various phenomena and carries out an impartial comparison of major world religions. She writes: "The work now submitted to public judgement is... meant to do justice and to speak the truth alike without malice or prejudice. Men and parties, and schools are but ephemera. Truth alone is eternal." Hence, the motto of the Theosophical Society: "There is no religion higher than truth". Her object was to make religion scientific and science religious. She laid emphasis on practice of ethics and altruism. In his autobiography, Mahatma Gandhi writes that it was reading Madame Blavatsky's *the Key to Theosophy* that stimulated in me the desire to read book on Hinduism (Parker, 2002).

Gandhi's life was a saga of experiments with truth. Truth that he sought revised in the human condition and in action. Gandhi had never looked at India as an entity apart from the world. For example, once he said, "What I have done will endure, not what I have said and written". This is understandable because it was addressed to his countrymen who are inclined to indulge in "celebral" activities resulting in words but no action. Although in 1930s, he said that once in parts of the world there had developed the opposite cults of action without rational thought. Gandhi's concept is articulated around the matrix of unity in diversity of social forces phenomena.

Philosophy has a conceptual framework, which implies a

unity of design either as a hypothesis or as a utopian construct. Gandhi's social philosophy is not merely a theoretical conceptual design. It's exploratory, rather than its explanatory character is more evident in it. Its meaning-system is a design for social living and its significance lies in man's endless research for truth or rather truthful human existence in world of conflict and change. (Ganguli, 1973, pp. 435 and 437)

It is widely believed that the September 11, 2001, terrorist attacks have changed the world dramatically, that nothing will be the same as the world enters into an age of terror. In America, a deeper self-examination is going on all over. Love, family and faith are re-emerging. The new appreciation for time spent with those they love poses a great spiritual question to materialistic supplies and workaholic careerist, and the new question is this: "What your life before September 11 really working for you? To many the answer is no. We once heard by a CEO who spoke at his retirement dinner to a group of Young executives. He said "I know you want my job, and I will tell you how to get it. Last week my daughter was married, and as she walked down the Isle, I realised I did not know the name of her best friend, or the last book she read, or her favourite colour. That is the price I paid for this job. If you want to pay the price you can have it." (Gellman, 2002, pp. 35-36).

People are figuring out the price that they have been paying for their lives, and for many it's just too damn high. We asked kids during December to name the very best they could receive. Their answer took our breath away. The overwhelming choice was: "More time with my mum and dad."

There is a lot of talk about spirituality now a day. Often it means: "I am not a part of any organised religion." We are telling people to give that old time religion another good look. The American clergy have done a great thing for God and for country in the last months… people have come home to faith. (Gellman, 2002, pp. 35-36)

There is a teaching in the Jewish faith that is also reflected in an African and Indian proverb "Sticks in a bundle are unbreakable but sticks alone can be broken by a child." Therefore, people need to be united and their unity would protect them best if they are bigger than just their family and small circle of friends. Every one needs a place to go, which is neither his/her home nor a place of work, where there can be a sense of unity and togetherness among people who likewise are seekers of or in need of hope. The ways of people finding God are almost the same as the ways they find each other (Gellman, 2002, pp. 35-36). This will give true meaning to life and abundance of hope rather than despair.

Let me narrate an incident told to me by late Prof. Usha Mehta, a freedom fighter. She said, "Once a group of farmers in the USA went to New York and stayed in the 80th floor in a posh hotel. One day, when they went out shopping and came back with a heavy load of gifts parcel, they found that the lift (elevator) was not working. So they had to climb up and they decided that while climbing the stairs each one would tell his talk of woes by turns. All of them did so but the one whose turn it was to tell the story while climbing the last 80th floor was little hesitant. All his colleagues assured him that they were to share his woes. He replied, "You are right. My tale of woes is not only mine, it is ours because you were good enough to trust me and hand over the bunch of keys to me when we went out. Now, while climbing the 80th floor I realised that I had forgotten the bunch of keys on the ground floor.

Hearing this Vinoba Bhave is reported to have reacted thus, "By all means go ahead in making progress in science. Go not only to 80th floor but to the 800th floor, to the moon and its floor *i.e.*, preserve our eternal and perennial values". (Mehta, 2001)

It will be helpful to reproduce some incidents from the autobiography of Gandhi which influenced his life (Gandhi, 1992).

1. Gandhi writes that, "There is an incident which occurred at the examination during my first year at the high school which is worth recording.
   Mr. Giles, the Educational Inspector, had come on a visit of inspection. He had set us give two words as a spelling exercise. One of the words was "Kettle". I

misspelt it. The teacher tried to prompt me with the point of his boot, but I would not be prompted. It was beyond me to see that she wanted me to copy the spelling from my neighbour's slate, for I had thought that the teacher was there to supervise against copying. The result was that all the boys except myself, were found to have spelt every word correctly. Only I had been stupid. The teacher tried later to bring this stupidity home to me but without effect. I could never learn the art of "copying": Yet the incident in the least diminishes my respect for any teacher. I was by nature blind to the fault of elders.

2. Some how my eyes fell on a book purchased by my father. It was Shravana Pitribhakti Natak, a play about Shravana's devotion to his parents. I read it with intense interest. There came to our place about the same time itinerant showmen. One of the picture I was shown was of Shravana carrying, by means of signs fitted for his shoulders, his blind parents on a pilgrimage. The book and the picture left an indelible impression on my mind. Here is an example for you to copy, I said to myself. The agonised lament of the parents over Shravanas' death is still fresh in my memory.
3. There was a similar incident connected with another play. Just about this time I had secured my father's permission to see a play performed by a certain dramatic company. The play — Harishchandra — captured my heart. I could never be tired of seeing it. But how often should I be permitted to go? It haunted me and I must have acted Harishchandra to myself times without number. "Why should not all be truthful like Harishchandra?" was the question I asked myself day and night. To follow truth and to go through all the ideals Harishchandra went through was the one ideal that inspired me. I literally believed in the sort of Harishchandra. The thought of it all often made me weep.

Thus, the socialisation process through which he had gone in his childhood made him a complete devotee to truth.

An inspiring practical lesson from *Mahabharat* is worth recalling:

Once the teacher Dronacharya, taught a lesson to the Kauravas and the Pandavas, "speak Truth, Observe your Dharma, and never idle in your Intellectual Pursuits." He directed the students to learn the lesson well. All the students went back home after the class.

The next day Dronacharya asked his students, "Have you learnt the lesson"? Each one enthusiastically replied that he had learnt his lesson well as he had just three sentences to be learnt. Yudhisthira, however begged the teacher's forgiveness as he had not learnt the lesson. The teacher was more surprised than displeased at this. He warned Yudhisthira to do his home work regularly. He asked him to learn the lesson well by the next day.

The next day too, Yudhishthira has not learnt the lesson. The same story was repeated on the third and the fourth day. By the fifth day, however, he appeared to have done his lesson. In a cheerful mood he went close to the teacher and said, "Sir, I have thoroughly learnt the lesson as I could understand its importance only today. The teacher asked him to repeat the sentence and wanted to know why he had taken so long to learn so small a lesson. Yudhishthira replied calmly, "Sir, I did try my best but failed." At times I had been telling a lie out of sheer carelessness and sometimes out of light heartedness. But since yesterday, I have neither spoken any lies, nor have I acted wrongly or thought wickedly. Therefore today I can say with confidence that I have learnt my lesson."

The teacher was amazed at this disclosure of Yudhishthira and said: you are really great. You've even excelled your teacher. You have taught me the right way as to how a lesson should be learnt. Hitherto I have made students to memorise lessons. I gave them just moral meanings so as to explain things to them. But a teacher should become a part of a student's mind and personality and should help him in his practical life. This side of teaching has so far been overlooked by me altogether.

The earth will be a veritable heaven if all of us learn our lesson the way you have done (Kapoor, 1995).

Would the present day teachers and students emulate this example?

Gandhi said, "I have always felt that the textbook for the pupil is his teacher. How was the spiritual training to be given? I made the children memorize and recite hymns, and read to them books on moral training. But that was far from satisfying me. As I came into closer contact with them (children) I saw that it was not through books that one could impart training of the spirit. Just as physical training was to be imparted through physical exercise and intellectual through intellectual exercise, even so the training of spirit was possible only through the exercise of spirit which entirely depends on the life and character of the teacher situated miles away to affect the spirit (moral) of the pupils by his way of living. It would be idle for me, if I were a liar, to teach boys to tell truth. A cowardly teacher would never succeed in making his students valiant, and stranger to self-restraint could never teach his pupils the value of self-restraint. I saw, therefore, that I must be an eternal object lesson to the boys and girls living with me. They thus became my teachers and I learnt to be good and live straight, if only for other's sake. I may say that the increasing discipline and restraint I imposed on myself at Tolstoy farm was mostly due to those wards of mine" (Gandhi, 1992, pp. 282-84).

Let us conclude: Gandhi's meaning is found in the first verse of Isha Upanishad, which says, "Covet not anybody's wealth". It could very well be a moral injunction against the possessiveness and greed of a hedonistic society. Gandhi, in fact, interpreted the term "renunciation" through the absorption of individual property into collective property.

Vrihadaranayaka Upanishad also contained three remarkable commandments: (1) Cultivate self-control; (2) Be generous and (3) Show compassion. The first was addressed to the gods who are drunk with power, the second, to the common men who are selfish and greedy; and the third, to the demons who are violent and destructive. Each group has the character of the other partially and potentially; but the dominant trait is heightened in each. Thus God could be selfish, greedy, violent and vindictive, but their heightened character is that of being power-mad. The common man could be power-mad as well as violent and destructive (partially and potentially) but his heightened character is that of being selfish and greedy. Similarly, the demons are power-mad, selfish and greedy (partially and not potentially), but the dominant character is that of being violent and destructive. If the dominant character of each group is curbed by each following the commandments addressed to it, there can be social peace. In his life time, Gandhi had to deal with gods and demons (metaphorically speaking) and with the common men. His percepts, as a votary of peace and non-violence, bear a striking resemblance to the commandments of the Vrihadaranayak Upanishad.

Salvation of modern society lies in following the commandments discussed above. Truth in a much wider sense means truth in thought, truth in speech and truth in action. Where there is truth, there is true knowledge, religious harmony, peace and bliss (*Ananda*). The Upanishad has wonderfully said, "The face of Truth is hidden behind the golden veil of Maya."

Faith, as embodied in religion, and reason as embodied in science are often erroneously thought of being in opposition to each other. Science is not an enemy of religion, only of superstition. Both science and religion are engaged in the search for truth, the main difference lies in the methodologies used. Science is an investigation of truth in the finite nature outside, the object. Religion is an investigation into the nature of infinite, the subject. Science aims for universally verifiable knowledge. Religion aims for individual realisation. It is true that universal laws operate regardless of one's belief and faith. We respect science, because it is premised on reason. (Anurag, 2002)

Without practical application, religion is of little value. Experimentation with religion is unique as the results take place right inside you. Truthfulness is the spiritual principle recommended for experimentation. Yoganandji says: truth is always wholesome. Giving happiness to others is vital to one's own happiness. The world outside is an extension of the world inside. So we should practice self-control, forgiveness and communion with God in our daily life. (Anurag, 2002, p. 16)

Buddha, looking deep, saw the thorns, which grow upon the road of life. He began meditating on "the disease" of life to find out what its sources are and whence its remedy could come. It must remove suffering by taking the noble eightfold path: (1) Right views; (2) Right aspiration; (3) Right speech; (4) Right conduct; (5) Right livelihood; (6) Right thought; (7) Right endeavours; and (8) Right contemplation.

Gandhi postulated eleven principles to solve the riddle of life: (1) Truth; (2) Non-violence; (3) Non-stealing; (4) Chastity; (5) Non-possession; (6) Physical labour; (7) Control of the palate; (8) Fearlessness; (9) Equality of all Religions; (10) Swadeshi; (11) Discarding of untouchability. The first five of these are the basic moral principles of Hinduism and Jainism. The six others are their derivatives suited to the requirements of the times.

Gandhi insists on holding on to the relative Truth, as long as the Absolute truth is beyond the reach of man. His search for truth must proceed in the community, which he is a part of. We may not know God, but we know his creation. Service of his creation is the service of God. In his quest of ultimate Truth he singles out courage as the crucial virtue, which people must show. This fearlessness is freedom from all external fear, fear of disease, bodily injury and death, of dispossession, of losing one's nearest and dearest, of losing reticulation, of giving offence.

Gandhi conceived the relationship between the individual and the society as analogous to that between the drops and the ocean. The drops while they can claim individuality cannot survive without the ocean and the ocean will lose its identity without the drops. He firmly believed that what he preached and professed after careful experimenting and meticulous practice was the truth, which could be relied on. His ideas, which came to be known as his philosophy, doctrine, principles or ideals, were in fact, as he admitted several times, part of his relentless search for the Truth. He stoutly believed that violence was not necessary to support the case of Truth, as it is inherently strong and capable of supporting itself. He was of firm view that the basic of all religions in the world was the law of love.

This scope of Truth according to Gandhi was not only the utterances of Truth. But he meant by it the observance of Truth by thought, word, and deed. A comprehensive understanding and sincere observance of Truth makes men so enlightened that there would not be anything which they would not understand. The implication is that Truth is knowledge and virtue. Conscience to Gandhi was higher than the highest court of the land. He believed that civilisation in the real sense of the term is not in the multiplication but in the deliberate and voluntary restriction of wants.

Wealth, material prosperity, and power are final objectives of the present day individual. Today's individual, who lives in atomized families, is more inward-looking than the individual of any previous generation. Truth, moral, and civic virtues, which are essential qualities for a man, do not have any significance in the modern society. The present day individual is shrewd enough to use all of them according to necessity, but at the same time does not attach any specific importance to them. In the present society, generally, the objectives are of pecuniary nature or related to power, position, or material benefits. While Gandhi advocated good means for good ends for individual of today, in general any means is acceptable if it is capable of achieving the desired objectives, which also may not be good or rational. The discourse of the modern civilisation is acquisition of wealth and comforts or luxuries as much as possible. For the individual of today, values and morality are not very much relevant, a share in the power and wealth become more important consideration for his allegiance to the state. Everything in the present civilisation and political system throughout the world is judged on the basis of publicity rather on the basis of facts that is truth.

Gandhi's mind proceeds through successive experiments into action and he follows a straight line. But he never stops. Anyone would risk error, especially when one would try to judge him merely on the basis of what he said ten years ago. It would be more so because his thought was in a constant process of evolution. An example may suffice here, that gives a glimpse of what were his characteristic.

"He was requested to define what he understood by God. He explained how, among the noblest attributes which the Hindu scriptures ascribed to God, he had in his youth chosen the word "Truth" an almost truly defining the essential element. He has said: "God is Truth". "But he added, "two years ago I advanced another steps, I now say, "Truth is God." For even the atheist do not doubt the necessity for the power of Truth. In their passion for discovering the Truth, the atheist have not hesitated to deny the existence of God, and, from their point of view, they are right. The seeker after Truth has heart tender as the Lotus, and hard as granite." (D.G. Tendulkar, Vol. III, pp. 181-183).

Gandhi described himself as a seeker after Truth. He believed that one should seek and follow truth in every field of life. One could pursue the quest of truth only if one had a scientific temper, and was willing to experiment and go by evidence. He, therefore, conducted experiments in every field of life. He started experimenting with his diet as early as his student day in London. He continued his experiments in South Africa, and later in India. He encouraged his friends and colleagues to conduct experiments, and asked them to be meticulous in controlling the conditions of experiments, observing and recording effects and submitting them to scrutiny.

REFERENCES

Singhvi, L.M., "The Credo of Tolerance", *The Hindustan Times*, September 11, 2002, New Delhi, p. 12.

The Hindustan Times, Editorial from Hiroshima to 9/11, *The Hindustan Times*, September 11, 2002, New Delhi p. 12.

Singhvi, L.M., "Universal Acceptance for Lasting Peace", *The Times of India*, September 11, 2002, New Delhi, p. 14.

Sharma, Arvind, Truth is Relative, *Gandhi Marg*, Vol. XXIV, No.1, April-June, 2002, pp. 95-98.

Gangrade K.D. *Religion and Peace — A Gandhian Perspective*, Gandhi Smriti and Darshan Samiti, New Delhi, 2001, pp. 45-53 and 56-57.

Vajpeyi Kailash, "Save Your Spirit from Technology", *The Times of India*, Sept. 12, 2002, p. 14.

Ganguli, B.N., *Gandhi's Social Philosophy — Perspective and Relevance*, Vikas Publishing House Pvt. Ltd., Delhi, 1973, p. 1.

Parkar, R.D., "Speaking the Truth without malice," *The Times of India*, September 13, 2002, New Delhi, p. 14.

Ganguli, B.N., *Gandhi's Social Philosophy–Perspective and Relevance*, Vikas Publishing House Pvt. Ltd. Delhi, 1973, pp. 435, 437.

Gellman Rabbi Mare & Hartman Monsignor Tom, "How Do You Find God", *Readers Digest*, Vol. 161, No. 963, July 2002, India, p. 36.

Mehta, Usha, Gandhi's Purifying Influence, *Gandhi Prasang*, Vol. III, No. 2, Jan. 30, 2001, pp. 86-91.

Gandhi, M.K., *An Autobiography — The Story of My Experiments with Truth*, Navajivan Publishing House, Ahmedabad (Translated from the Gujrati by Mahadev Desai), edition Feb., 1992, pp. 5-6.

Kapoor, N.D., *Fragrance of Life*, Vishwa Jagriti Mission, New Delhi, 1995, pp. 21-22.

Gandhi, M.K., *An Autobiography*, Navajivan Press, Ahmedabad, (edition) 1992, pp. 282-84.

Anurag, "No Conflict Between Faith and Reason", *The Times of India*, August 14, 2002, New Delhi, p. 16.

Part II

4

Biographical Note on Dr. D.S. Kothari

Born	July 6, 1906 at Udaipur, Rajasthan	
Education	Matric, Rajputana Board	1922
	Intermediate, Rajputana Board	1924
	B.Sc., Allahabad University	1926
	M.Sc., Allahabad University	1928
	Ph.D., Cambridge University	1933
Married	Jan.1925 to Sujan Kunwar (neé Surana)	
1934-42	Reader in Physics and Head of the Department, University of Delhi.	
1942-48	Professor and Head, Department of Physics, University of Delhi.	
1944	President of the Physics Section of Indian Science Congress.	
1948-61	Professor of Physics, Delhi University.	
1948-51	Scientific Advisor, Minister of Defence, Government of India.	
1951-61	Scientific Advisor (Honorary), Minister of Defence, Government of India; Head Department of Physics, Delhi University.	
1960-64	Chairman, Commission for Scientific and Technical Terminology, Government of India.	
1961-73	Chairman, University Grants Commission	
1962	Awarded Padma Bhushan	
1963	General President, Indian Science Congress	
1964-66	Chairman, Education Commission	
1971-93	Emeritus Professor of Physics, University of Delhi.	
1973	Awarded Padma Vibhushan	

1973-74	President, Indian National Science Academy
1974-76	Chairman, UPSC Committee on Recruitment Policy and Selection Methods.
1982-92	Chancellor, Jawaharlal Nehru University
Died	February 4, 1993 at Jaipur, Rajasthan.

Professor D.S. Kothari was a renowned physicist and a deep thinker. Apart from Heading the Department of Physics of Delhi University for a number of years, he served as the Scientific Advisor to the Minister of Defence for almost 13 years and as the Chairman of the University Grants Commission for 12 years. By his dedication and foresight he was able to transform a University Department that was teaching physics only to B.Sc (General) students, into a world renowned research Centre. He also helped to establish a wide network of research laboratories around the country for the Defence Research and Development Organisation (DRDO), starting from scratch.

Professor Kothari was also a deeply religious person, with profound knowledge of ancient Indian thought. Though in school he studied Urdu and Persian and had very poor knowledge of Hindi, after retirement he studied Sanskrit and was soon quoting the Gita and other scriptures. He was convinced that science and religion do not contradict each other, but rather complement each other. Science deals with the external world of space and time, and of matter and energy, while religion deals with the inner world of the Self or 'I'. Both are search for Truth, but in different domains.

Dr. Kothari wrote extensively and gave several invited lectures to university teachers and students, as well as to Fellows of various science Academies on Science and Ethics, Atom and Self. He advocated that anything anti-science must be totally unacceptable, but that there are many things beyond science — those dealing with the inner world, in which science has nothing to say.

The Principle of Complementarity which we owe to Niels Bohr, is perhaps, the most significant and revolutionary concept of modern physics. The complementarity approach can enable people to see that seemingly irreconcilable points of view need not be contradictory. According to Dr. Kothari, 'the most profound, rich and fundamental of all complementarities is that of *matter* (brain) and *consciousness* (mind).' He was amongst the few who understood and tried to explain that 'the core of ethical — spiritual insights propounded by the Upanishads, Buddhism and Jainism rest essentially on the complementarity approach.' He talked extensively of Syadvada (Jain formalism of complementarity), and explained how this approach enriches our understanding of complementarity in physics. He emphasised in a number of his lectures that 'Man's future belongs to *ahimsa* and *science*.'

Such a rare individual who synthesised the deepest thoughts of science and of life, was born in a school teacher's family in Udaipur on 6th July 1906. Both his father and grandfather passed away when he was barely twelve years of age. He was brought up by his mother, who was a devout Jain and a generous lady — always willing to help others in need. She strongly believed in *aparigrah*, not keeping things that are not essential. These qualities of his mother shaped his character. When Prof. Kothari was awarded the Anuvrat Award carrying a cash award of Rs.1,00,000, he felt he did not need it and most politely declined to accept it.

To help Daulat Singh to continue his studies, Sir Siremal Bapna, an old friend of his father and the Chief Minister of Indore State, took him to Indore. Staying with Sir Siremal and his family, Daulat Singh completed his Matriculation and then for his Intermediate moved back to Udaipur. He topped in the Rajasthan Board and was awarded a scholarship by the Maharana of Mewar for further studies. The gesture of Sir Siremal in recognising and nurturing talent left a deep impression on Kothari. When he was in a position to take decisions, he got introduced the Science Talent Search Scheme by National Council for Educational Research and Training (NCERT), which supported talented students right upto their Ph.D. degree. The scheme is still continuing, though in a greatly modified form. He also introduced the Young Scientists Awards in the Indian National Science Academy, when he was its President (1973-74).

After his Intermediate examination, Daulat Singh joined Agra College for B.Sc. Here he was not very happy and one morning an old friend and a senior student of Allahabad University, Shri Laxmi Lal Joshi dropped in to meet him. He advised him to come to Allahabad because of Prof. M.N. Saha being there. Daulat Singh expressed his inability to do that since he had deposited all fees at Agra College and he had no further money left. On insistence by Shri Joshi, Daulat Singh met the Principal of the College — an Englishman, and told him of his desire to move to Allahabad. The Principal consented to his moving to Allahabad University which had already made a name for itself in the sciences. Further, being impressed by the keen desire of young Kothari to persue science, he ordered the refund of all fees, as a special case. In later life, Dr. Kothari was always willing to help the really needy, even if he had to go a little out of the normal way.

In 1925, Dr. Kothari was married to Sujan Kunwar (neé Surana). Theirs was a happy married life and in true Indian tradition Mrs. Kothari relieved him of all the worries of the household. She was extremely hospitable and many visitors, including Prof. D.V. Gogate, Prof. M.N. Saha and others spent weeks and months with the Kothari family.

At Allahabad University he soon became one of the most favourite students of Prof. Meghnad Saha. After passing M.Sc. in 1928 with first position in the class, he was awarded U.P. State Government Scholarship to go to England. On reaching England in September 1930, he was informed by the office of the High Commission that he had been admitted to Oxford and admission in Cambridge was totally out of question. Kothari was greatly disappointed. As luck would have it, one of his friends from Udaipur — Mr. Gulam Ali, met him and told him that he will be visiting Cambridge next Sunday. Kothari felt an urge at least to visit and see Cambridge University. On arriving in Cambridge both friends went to see the Cavendish Laboratory, which they thought would anyway be closed, being a Sunday. On entering the building, they were met by a lady who enquired about the purpose of their visit. On mentioning the name of Rutherford, the lady took them immediately to the Library where Lord Rutherford was sitting and reading a journal. Kothari was dumb-founded. Gathering courage he hesitatingly said: 'Sir, my teacher Prof. M.N. Saha from Allahabad University had written to you about me. I am Daulat Singh Kothari.'. 'Oh, Mr. Kothari I am reading your paper right now. It is very interesting. Have you finished all the admission formalities? If not, please complete them soon. My secretary will help you'. And so he was admitted to Cavendish Laboratory inspite of the initial reluctance of the High Commission Office.

Learning from this experience, Dr. Kothari was always available to his students and staff. He would say that if one properly utilised ones time, there was enough time even to play with grand-children. He would go to sleep daily at 9.00 p.m.

He obtained his Ph.D. degree from Cambridge University with Lord Rutherford as his supervisor. In 1934 he joined Delhi University as Reader and Head of the Physics Department and his association with this University continues to this day. When he died on February 4, 1993, he was Emeritus Professor and later the University named one of its Post Graduate Hostels after him.

When Dr. Kothari, joined the University, it imparted education only up to B.Sc. level. Due to his foresight and devotion to work, soon the Physics Department acquired a position on the world map, both for teaching and research. It may be recalled that at that time on the teaching staff were Professors R.C. Majumdar, F.C. Auluck, P.K. Kichlu, N.K. Saha, P.L. Kapur and young lecturers K.S. Singwi, A.R. Verma and R.P. Bambha and others. In this the contribution of the then Vice-Chancellor, Sir Maurice Gwyer who had great faith in Dr. Kothari, cannot be underestimated. He was a very dynamic person. He believed that 'one should select a man wisely and trust him boldly.' He would further advise that 'one should never be generous at public expense'. These are some of the lessons Dr. Kothari accepted and followed in his life.

From 1948 to 1961 he served as Scientific Advisor to the Minister of Defence. About his work during this period Mr. Nagaratnam, one of the very Senior Defence Scientists records:

'The Nation owes a deep debt of gratitude to Professor Kothari for the foundation he laid for the healthy development and growth of defence science in the country'.

After the explosion of two atom bombs over Japan in 1945 (one on August 6 and another on August 9), Dr. Kothari gave two lectures on the possible mechanism of these devices, one to a general audience and another to military officers. These were very highly appreciated. At that time all information about fission and nuclear energy was classified and treated as highly secret. In spite of this, from the little information available from research papers published in scientific journals and his own depth of thinking, he succeeded in working out a model for explaining the release of energy in atom bombs. Following this, Pandit Nehru asked him and Dr. H.J. Bhabha to write a book on this topic. The entire task was undertaken by Dr. Kothari and the book 'Nuclear Explosions and Their Effects' was published by the Government of India in 1956. An enlarged second edition appeared in 1958. The book received highly complimentary reviews and was translated into Russian, German and Japanese (but not in Hindi or any other Indian language).

Dr. R.E. Lapp, while writing about the book in Bulletin of the Atomic Scientists (USA) (December 1956 issue), stated: 'The apparent ease with which the Indian physicists diagnosed the structure of US weapons should be of interest and concern to our Atomic Energy Commission and Central Intelligence Agency. Indeed, the publication of some of the weapons data should encourage a bolder declassification policy by AEC and Defence Department. It is to be hoped that the forthcoming US Effect of Nuclear Weapons will be as complete as the Indian account of the high-yield weapons.'

The preface to the German translation said " Thus with the publication of the Indian book, a work has come out which makes history...... history-making books are those which convey decisive knowledge at the right moment in an authentic form — unobjectionable and incorruptible, objective, consolidated and total — as the basis for the thoughts and actions of citizens and even of statesmen.'

For almost 12 years Dr. Kothari served the University

Grants Commission as its Chairman. He desired that the country must have some research centres in different fields of study, which would compare with outstanding centres of learning anywhere in the world. With this in mind he created a number of 'Centre of Advanced Studies' in several Universities. He also helped to organise quite a few bi-national Conferences devoted to improving teaching of different science subjects in colleges and universities. He Chaired the Education Commission (1964-66) which presented its Report in 1966. It 'was hailed as a landmark in educational development in India and other developing countries'.

He strongly felt that for any nation to progress, all education must be in the mother tongue of the child. For teaching sciences, proper terminology in regional languages becomes essential. He persuaded the Government to set up a Commission for Scientific and Technical Terminology and he was appointed its first Chairman. He also guided the policies of UPSC, NCERT and quite a few other organisations.

Prof. Kothari's life was greatly influenced by his remarkable teacher, Prof. M.N. Saha, a person with phenomenal memory and very simple life style. This strong bond of *guru-shishya* relationship continued for life.

Dr. Kothari was an original thinker and a great human being. His approach to problems was always novel. Once during discussions he was asked for his views on how burning of public property like buses and railway stations by mobs could be prevented. He replied: 'No one burns his own property. The Government utilities do not serve the people so well as to make them feel that these belong to them. We must search our own hearts'.

One was amazed to see a lot of people coming to him for advice regarding all kinds of problems. He once explained that very often people give advice from their own point of view, which is not right. We must give advice after considering the point of view of the person who has come to seek advice.

He retained a child like curiosity to learn and remained a diligent student all his life. Because so much appears in print these days, he would advise people to read only the 'Masters'.

After his retirement from the UGC in 1973 (at the age of 67 years) he decided to read the Gita in the original. In school he had learnt Urdu and Persian and could not even write Hindi correctly. In spite of this, within a couple of years he was able to read and explain in depth the *shlokas* of the Gita and recite them also. Because of his deep understanding of physics he was able to see and appreciate its close links with ancient Indian thoughts. Many outstanding foreign scientists and thinkers, when visiting India would come and meet Dr. Kothari. They would discuss philosophical and scientific questions and were impressed by his depth of understanding. They became his admirers and life-long fridends. Among them were Nobel Laureates P.M.S. Blackett, P. Kapitza, S.Chandrasekhar, I. Prigogine, George Wald and others. While dedicating his book '*Meaning and Medicine*' (Bantam Books, New York, 1991) to him, Dr. Larry Dossey MD (U.S.A.), wrote: 'Dr. Kothari spoke the languages of modern physics and the ancient Upanishads with equal profundity and grace. In his life and philosophy he has honoured the realities of the physical, mental and the spiritual as few scientists I have known.' On learning of his death George Wald, Nobel Laureate wrote: 'He is a person I loved and enormously appreciated more directly than any other Indian I came to know; a superb scientist with a warm soul'.

Now he is physically no more with us. However he will continue to live through his writings. A Collection of the Convocation Addresses which he delivered at various Universities around the country have been collected by Prof. D.S. Kothari Centre for Science, Ethics and Education (KCSEE) of the University of Delhi and published by National Institute of Science Communication (NISCOM), CSIR, New Delhi. His Memorial and Medal Lectures have been published under the title 'Atom and Self' while his Lectures on Higher Education, and Defence Research have been brought out under the title 'Knowledge and Wisdom', (publisher New Age International (P) Ltd., New Delhi).

5

On Particle and Wave Nature of Matter and the Complementarity of the Two Aspects*

Being a Conversation between a Classical Physicist and a Quantum Theorist

Classical Physicist: Mr. Quantum Theorist! You are so fond of talking always about *Duality, uncertainty, ψ, Φ,* and so on. Can you tell me in plain words what is really new in these things? Do you not see that Duality is everywhere? Take the two faces of a coin, the two sides of a shield, and so on. What wonder is there if photons and electrons also show a dual nature, *particles at times and waves at other times*?

Quantum Theorist: You will excuse me if I talk a bit of philosophy. How do you know, Mr. C.P., that a coin has two faces? I only see one face at a time. It may be that it is the same face which at times shows a head and at other times (perhaps miraculously) changes into a tail. How do you refute me?

Classical Physicist: Well, I show you both the faces at the same time. Put a mirror behind and you see the two faces *simultaneously— the dual aspect seen together.*

Quantum Theorist: You have hit at the crucial point; and it is that you can arrange an experiment where you can see the dual aspect of a coin, a shield, etc., at the same time; and also one can so arrange that the one aspect gradually and continuously passes into the other aspect. Having seen the two aspects together one can easily construct a picture of the whole entity. But what will happen when the entity is such that, with

* Science and Culture, Vol. 2, No. 3, September 1936.

all the ingenuity one can command, one cannot arrange an experiment which will show us its two aspects at the same time. Imagine a coin, call it X, for which we can see one face at a time but *under no circumstances* its two faces at the same time.

Classical Physicist: You seem to be talking nonsense. If a man has common-sense, and he will be no classical physicist if he has not that, he would refuse to imagine such fantastic things.

Quantum Theorist: I wonder if the classical physicist has much of commonsense. He has only a naive faith. As for commonsense it has never been his strong point. Fancy your very first law of motion asserting that a particle unacted by force moves in a straight line with uniform velocity. Now, if I ask you to draw an exact straight line you yourself will agree that it will be an impossible task. Make your best efforts and yet the line will always show some unevenness, probably not to the naked eye but under a microscope. You cannot draw a perfect straight line with all your instruments and twentieth-century experimental technique, and yet you believe that an insignificant and inanimate tiny particle can perform this miracle. If it is not faith, I wonder what it is! But I have digressed from the main point.

I was asking you to imagine a coin which possesses the strange property that we can see only its one face at a time and find it impossible to devise any means whereby we could see both the faces simultaneously. Such a coin, fortunately, never exists. If it ever existed we shall soon say it was a ghost, for we could never from a *picture* of a coin with such ghost-like properties. No one will say it was a coin. All will say it was a ghost.

Classical Physicist: But what has Quantum theory to do with such ghost-like coins?

Quantum Theorist: If there was no connection between the two I should hardly talk of it. But I shall narrate you a short story before I disclose their relation to Quantum theory. The story is about one Mr. H. who lives in *Quantumland* — the 'land' discovered by Bohr, Heisenberg, Dirac, and others.

Classical Physicist: Oh yes! I have heard of *Quantumland*. It is quite a fashionable land these days. Most of the modern physicists have their headquarters there.

Quantum Theorist: If you are interested, I can tell you something more about this land and its recent developments. Planck was the first who entered this land, but Einstein and Bohr soon joined him. Bohr has done most in making this land fertile. Most of it at present is being cultivated by his disciples — he adding from time to time new fertilizers, but the yield as yet is not enough to satisfy all the demands.* You must have heard that Eddington has built there a sky-scraper of 136 stories, and later added one more to make the total 137. Dirac has proved that his house is spinning. But you cannot observe the spin. The most popular game in that land is that of "billiards" and Rutherford has ever been the champion. The game is very different from ordinary billiards and Rutherford and his co-players are continually finding new kinds of balls to play the game. You can easily recognize the houses of de Broglie and Schrödinger by their wavelike structure. Heisenberg has a castle closed on all sides and having no windows or even doors — it is a wonder how he himself gets in and out. If we believe Gamow, then he does this by 'leaking' through the solid walls. At one time Compton was the minister for justice — and he was a merciful judge. He punished quanta according to their size. For the same offence a bigger quantum was meted out more punishment than a smaller one. Raman is the present incumbent of this office — he punishes quanta to the same extent no matter whether the quantum is big or

---

* A conference on atomic physics was held at Copenhagen on June 17-20 this year at Prof. Bohr's Institute for theoretical physics. About eighty physicists attended the discussions. A brief report has appeared in *Nature* of July 4th, 1936, from which the following extract is taken :

"The course of the discussion was, as always, directed by the masterly fundamental criticisms of Bohr. On these occasions, when so many able theorists are gathered together, it is clear that Bohr's physical insight is the power which contributes most to the advances of theoretical atomic physics, and creates the conditions which fertilize the mathematical abilities of theoretical workers elsewhere...

The general impression left by the conference was that progress in experimental research on the atomic nucleus is very rapid, but that the advance in the theoretical description of the new results is much slower."

small.* The Surgeon-General is Saha. He has discovered a 'thermal' knife to operate upon atoms — the electrons in atoms can be most successfully amputated with this knife. He has shown us a method of diagnosing the condition of atoms in distant cosmic worlds and astrophysicists the world over now use his method. And there are one or two most distinguished visitors from other lands, *e.g.*, Milne from Cosmic land.

But let me now resume the story about Mr. H.

It has been found that whenever Mr. H has gone into a fruit garden in his native land some fruits have always disappeared. You will conclude that he is a thief, but if you are a conscientious person, you will for a while hesitate to draw that conclusion and ask the police to investigate the matter and catch the fellow red-handed, *i.e.*, actually stealing the fruits. The police did investigate the matter: policemen did themselves behind the trees and kept a secret watch on H. They used all the ingenuity of Scotland Yard to keep a watch as secret as possible so that H could not have the faintest clue that any policemen were keeping a watch on him. So fruits were stolen during this period, though the police saw H several times going in and out of the garden. They then retired and reported that H was not a thief. But after the police retired the old trouble started again — whenever H entered the garden, fruits always disappeared. Now I ask you, Mr. C.P., what will you call him — a thief or an honest person?

Classical Physicist: Mr. Q.T., from what you say I suspect that the fellow is not honest but some-how he succeeded in evading the police; possibly the police did not utilize all their resources in tracking him down.

Quantum Theorist: Take it as certain that the police spared no pains in this investigation. They used all their resources — photo-cells, wireless apparatus, infra red light, and so on, and took the help of all the physicists, chemists, engineers, and so on, yet on no account they found H in the actual act of stealing the fruits.

---

* In Compton effect the energy decrease of the incident quantum *i.e.* the difference between the energies of the incident and the scattered quanta is proportional to the energy of the incident quantum. In Raman effect, on the other hand, this energy difference is independent of the energy of the incident quantum.

Classical Physicist: I still suspect H to be a thief; only he seems to be cleverer than all the police and may be using some kind of secret rays (not known to the police) to know the presence of policemen watching his movement.

Quantum Theorist: Dear C. P.! what you are saying now does not do you justice as a physicist. A physicist, as you yourself have so often said, is not entitled to form opinions which are not ultimately warranted by observations and experiments. In the case of H one set of facts (police reports) show that he is honest; the other set of facts (report of the gardener) show him to be a thief, and as a physicist I see no reason why you should be prejudiced and give more weight to one set of facts than to the other.

Classical Physicist: This seems a bit puzzling. I will say that the fellow is no ordinary person.

Quantum Theorist: The actual facts about H are that he is sometimes a thief and sometimes honest, and so let us call him a thief—honest man. We cannot understand such a strange character, because it is one which is not met with in our ordinary experience. He is a "non-classical man" and therefore his behaviour cannot be comprehended on classical ideas. I now come to the relationship of these examples with the fundamental principles of Quantum Mechanics.

An electron or a photon, or as a matter of that any particle, has a dual nature; it sometimes behaves as a particle and sometimes as a wave, and the most fundamental point is that we can think of no possible experiment wherein the particle aspect and the wave aspect can both be seen at the same time. That precludes us from forming a mental picture or a model of electron, photon, etc. Just as with our ordinary human ideas we could not understand the behaviour of H in our second example, or could form the picture of the coin in the first example, similarly with classical concepts it is impossible to understand the nature of electrons, etc. We must emphasize once again that the cause of this impossibility is not the dual nature of the entities (electrons, photons, etc.) but this *complementarity of the particle and the wave aspects, i.e., the two aspects can never be seen at the same time*. If the two aspects could be demonstrated at the same time, then it would be possible for Classical Physics to form a picture of these entities on classical lines. Classical Physics fails to explain the behaviour of these entities because of the complementarity of these two aspects. As Dirac has remarked, the basic concepts of Quantum Physics can no longer be expressed in familiar language or in terms of words at all. "Nature works on a different plan. Her laws do not govern the world in any direct way, instead they control a sub-stratum of which we cannot form a mental picture without introducing irrelevancies." It is only by mathematical symbols that one can express, or better describe, the workings of Nature. As Jeans has said, "God seems to be a pure mathematician."

Next time when we meet again we shall invite a pure mathematician also at our conversation.

Classical Physicist: In my younger days I used to picture the electron as a Roman soldier. You can look straight into his face and he remains unperturbed. My habit of forming mental pictures of everything, I am afraid, still continue and now I may perhaps picture the electron as a tiny bird. You look at it and when you want to locate its distance from you, you throw a measuring tape, the distance is known, but lo! the bird is frightened and flies away and its velocity becomes unknown — Heisenberg's uncertainity principle, when the position is exactly known the velocity is completely unknown and when the velocity is exactly known the position is completely unknown. We cannot observe an electron without perturbing it and, as you have said, it is impossible to enquire closely as to how this disturbance arises or to know its exact amount.

6

Identity and Non-Identity*

Kūtadanta, the head of the Brahmans in the village of Dānamati having approached the Blessed One respectfully, greeted him and said: "I am told, O samana, that thou art the Buddha, the Holy One, the All-knowing, the Lord of the world. But if thou wert the Buddha, wouldst thou not come like a king in all thy glory and power?"

Said the Blessed One: "Thine eyes are holden. If the eye of thy mind were undimmed thou couldst see the glory and the power of truth."

Said Kūtadanta: "Show me the truth and I shall see it. But thy doctrine is without consistency. If it were consistent, it would stand; but as it is not, it will pass away."

The Blessed One replied: "The truth will never pass away."

Kūtadanta said: "I am told that thou teachest the law, yet thou tearest down religion. Thy disciples despise rites and abandon immolation, but reverence for the gods can be shown only by sacrifices. The very nature of religion consists in worship and sacrifices."

Said the Buddha: "Greater than the immolation of bullocks is the sacrifice of self. He who offers to the gods his evil desires will see the uselessness of slaughtering animals at the altar. Blood has no cleansing power but the eradication of lust will make the heart pure. Better than worshipping gods is obedience to the laws of righteousness."

Kūtadanta, being of a religious disposition and anxious about his fate after death, had sacrificed countless victims. Now he saw the folly of atonement by blood. Not yet satisfied,

* Paul Carus, *The Gospel of Buddha*, Pub. Division, 1990.

however, with the teaching of the Tathāgata, Kūtadanta continued: "Thou believest, O Master, that beings are reborn; that they migrate in the evolution of life; and that subject to the law of karma we must reap what we sow. Yet thou teachest the non-existence of the soul! Thy disciples praise utter self-extinction as the hightest bliss of Nirvāna. If I am merely a combination of the sankhāras, my existence will cease when I die. If I am merely a compound of sensations and ideas and desires, wither can I go at the dissolution of the body?"

Said the Blessed One: "O Brahman, thou art religious and earnest. Thou art seriously concerned about thy soul. Yet is thy work in vain because thou art lacking in the one thing that is needful.

"There is rebirth of character, but no transmigration of self. Thy thought-forms reappear, but there is no egoentity transferred. The stanza uttered by a teacher is reborn in the schollar who repeats the words.

"Only through ignorance and delusion do men indulge in the dream that their souls are separate and self-existent entities.

"Thy heart, O Brahman, is cleaving still to self; thou art anxious about heaven but thou seekest the pleasures of self in heaven, and thus thou canst not see the bliss of truth and the immortality of truth.

"Verily I say unto thee: The Blessed One has not come to teach death, but to teach life, and thou discernest not the nature of living and dying.

"This body will be dissolved and no amount of sacrifice will save it. Therefore, seek thou the life that is of the mind. Where self is, truth cannot be; yet when truth comes, self will disappear. Therefore, let thy mind rest in the truth; propagate the truth, put the whole will in it, and let it spread. In the truth thou shalt live for ever.

"Self is death and truth is life. The cleaving to self is a perpetual dying, while moving in the truth is partaking of Nirvāna which is life everlasting,"

Kūtadanta said: " Where, O venerable Master, is Nirvāna?"

"Nirvāna is wherever the precepts are obeyed," replied the Blessed One.

"Do I understand thee aright," rejoined the Brahman, "that Nirvāna is not a place, and being nowhere it is without reality?"

"Thou dost not understand me aright," said the Blessed One, "Now listen and answer these questions: Where does the wind dwell?"

"Nowhere," was the reply.

Buddha retorted: "Then, sir, there is no such thing as wind."

Kūtadanta made no reply; and the Blessed One asked again: "Answer me, O Brahman, where does wisdom dwell? Is wisdom a locality?"

"Wisdom has no allotted dwelling-place," replied Kūtadanta.

Said the Blessed One: "Meanest thou that there is no wisdom, no enlightenment, no righteousness, and no salvation, because Nirvāna is not a locality? As a great and mighty wind which passeth over the world in the heat of the day, so the Tathāgata comes to blow over the minds of mankind with the breath of his love, so cool, so sweet, so calm, so delicate; and those tormented by fever assuage their suffering and rejoice at the refreshing breeze."

Said Kūtadanta: "I feel, O Lord, that thou proclaimest a great doctrine, but I cannot grasp it. Forbear with me that I ask again: Tell me, O Lord, if there be no ātman, how can there be immortality? The activity of the mind passeth, and our thoughts are gone when we have done thinking."

Buddha replied: "Our thinking is gone, but our thoughts continue. Reasoning ceases, but knowledge remains."

Said Kūtadanta: "How is that? Is not reasoning and knowledge the same?"

The Blessed One explained the distinction by an illustration: "It is as when a man wants, during the night, to send a letter, and, after having his clerk called, has a lamp lit, and gets the letter written. Then, when that has been done, he extinguishes the lamp. But though the writing has been finished and the light has been put out the letter is still there. Thus does reasoning cease and knowledge remain; and in the same way mental activity ceases, but experience, wisdom, and all the fruits of our acts endure."

Kūtadanta continued: "Tell me, O Lord, pray tell me, where, if the sankhāras are dissolved, is the identity of my self. If my thoughts are propagated, and if my soul migrates, my thoughts cease to be *my* thoughts and my soul ceases to be *my* soul. Give me an illustration, but pray, O Lord, tell me, where is the identity of my self?"

Said the Blessed One: "Suppose a man were to light a lamp; would it burn the night through?"

"Yes, it might do so," was the reply.

"Now, is it the same flame that burns in the first watch of the night as in the second ?"

Kūtadanta hesitated. He thought "Yes, it is the same flame,"but fearing the complications of a hidden meaning, and trying to be exact, he said: "No, it is not."

"Then," continued the Blessed One, "there are flames, one in the first watch and the other in the second watch."

"No, sir, " said Kūtadanta. "In one sense it is not the same flame, but in another sense it is the same flame. It burns the same kind of oil, it emits the same kind of light, and it serves the same purpose."

"Very well," said the Buddha, "and would you call those flames the same that have burned yesterday and are burning now in the same lamp, filled with the same kind of oil, illuminating the same room?"

"They may have been extinguished during the day," suggested Kūtadanta.

Said the Blessed One: "Suppose the flame of the first watch had been extinguished during the second watch, would you call it the same if it burns again in the third watch?"

Replied Kūtadanta: "In one sense it is a different flame, in another it is not."

The Tathāgata asked again: "Has the time that elapsed during the extinction of the flame anything to do with its identity or non-identity?"

"No, sir," said the Brahman, "it has not. There is a difference and an identity, whether many years elapsed or only one second, and also whether the lamp has been extinguished in the meantime or not."

"Well, then, we agree that the flame of to-day is in a certain sense the same as the flame of yesterday, and in another sense it is different at every moment. Moreover, the flames of the same kind, illuminating with equal power the same kind of rooms are in a certain sense the same."

"Yes, sir," replied Kūtadanta.

The Blessed One continued: "Now, suppose there is a man who feels like thyself, thinks like thyself, and acts like thyself, is he not the same man as thou?"

"No, sir," interrupted Kūtadanta.

Said the Buddha: "Dost thou deny that the same logic holds good for thyself that holds good for the things of the world?"

Kūtadanta be thought himself and rejoined slowly: "No, I do not. The same logic holds good universally; but there is a peculiarity about my self which renders it altogether different from everything else and also from other selves. There may be another man who feels exactly like me, thinks like me, and acts like me; suppose even he had the same name and the same kind of possessions he would not be myself."

"True, Kūtadanta," answered Buddha, "he would not be thyself. Now, tell me, is the person who goes to school one, and that same person when he has finished his schooling another? Is it one who commits a crime, another who is punished by having his hands and feet cut off?"

"They are same," was the reply.

"Then sameness is constituted by continuity only?" asked the Tathāgata.

"Not only by continuity," said Kūtadanta," but also and mainly by identity of character."

"Very well," concluded the Buddha, "then thou agreest that persons can be the same, in the same sense as two flames of the same kind are called the same; and thou must recognize that in this sense another man of the same character and product of the same karma is the same as thou."

"Well, I do," said the Brahman.

The Buddha continued: "And in this same sense alone art thou the same to day as yesterday. Thy nature is not constituted by the matter of which thy body, of sensations, of thoughts. Thy person is the combination of the sankhāras. Wherever they are, thou art. Whithersoever they go, thou goest. Thus thou wilt recognize in a certain sense an identity of thy self, and in another sense a difference. But he who does not recognize the identity should deny all identity, and should say that the questioner is no longer the same person as he who a minute after receives the answer. Now consider the continuation of thy personality, which is preserved in thy karma. Dost thou call it death and annihilation, or life and continued life?"

"I call it life and continued life," rejoined Kūtadanta, "for it is the continuation of my existence, but I do not care for that kind of continuation. All I care for is the continuation of self in the other sense, which makes of every man, whether identical with me or not, an altogether different person."

"Very well," said Buddha. 'This is what thou desirest and this is the cleaving to self. This is thy error. All compound things are transitory: they grow and they decay. All compound things are subject to pain: they will be separated from what they love and be joined to what they abhor. All compound things lack a self, an ātman, an ego."

"How is that?" asked Kūtadanta.

"Where is thy self?" asked the Buddha. And when Kūtadanta made no reply, he continued: "Thy self to which thou cleavest is a constant change. Years ago thou wast a small babe; then, thou wast a boy; then a youth, and now, thou art a man. Is there any identity of the bale and the man? There is an identity in a certain sense only. Indeed there is more identity between the flames of the first and the third watch, even though the lamp might have been extinguished during the second watch. Now which is thy true self, that of yesterday, that of to-day, or that of to-morrow, for the preservation of which thou clamourest?"

Kūtadanta was bewildered. "Lord of the world," he said, "I see my error, but I am still confused."

The Tathāgata continued: "It is by a process of evolution that sankhāras come to be. There is no sankhāra which has sprung into being without a gradual becoming. Thy sankhāras are the product of thy deeds in former existences. The combination of thy sankhāras is thy self. Wheresoever they are impressed thither thy self migrates. In thy sankhāras thou wilt continue to live and thou wilt reap in future existences the harvest sown now and in the past."

"Verily, O Lord," rejoined Kūtadanta, "this is not a fair retribution. I cannot recognize the justice that others after me will reap what I am sowing now."

The Blessed One waited a moment and then replied: "Is all teaching in vain? Dost thou not understand that those others are thou thyself? Thou thyself wilt reap what thou sowest, not others.

"Think of a man who is ill-bred and destitute, suffering from the wretchedness of his condition. As a boy he was slothful and indolent, and when he grew up he had not learned a craft to earn a living. Wouldst thou say his misery is not the product of his own action, because the adult is no longer the same person as was the boy ?

"Verily, I say unto thee: Not in the heavens, not in the midst of the sea, not if thou hidest thyself away in the clefts of the mountains, wilt thou find a place where thou canst escape the fruit of thine evil actions.

"At the same time thou art sure to receive the blessings of thy good actions.

"The man who has long been travelling and who returns home in safety, the welcome of kinsfolk, friends, and acquaintances awaits. So, the fruits of his good works bid him welcome who has walked in the path of righteousness, when he passes over from the present life into the hereafter."

Kūtadanta said: 'I have faith in the glory and excellency of thy doctrines. My eye cannot as yet endure the light; but I now understand that there is no self, and the truth dawns upon me. Sacrifices cannot save, and invocations are idle talk. But how shall I find the path to life everlasting? I know all the Vedas by heart and have not found the truth."

Said the Buddha: "Learning is a good thing; but it availeth not. True wisdom can be acquired by practice only. Practise the truth that thy brother is the same as thou. Walk in the noble path of righteousness and thou wilt understand that while there is death in self, there is immortality in truth."

Said Kūtadanta: "Let me take my refuge in the Blessed One, in the Dharma, and in the brotherhood. Accept me as thy disciple and let me partake of the bliss of immortality."

7

My View of the World*

Suppose you are sitting on a bench beside a path in high mountain country. There are grassy slopes all around, with rocks trusting through them; on the opposite slope of the valley there is a stretch of scree with a low growth of alder bushes. Woods climb steeply on both sides of the valley, up to the line of treeless pasture; and facing you, soaring up from the depths of the valley, is the mighty, glacier-tipped peak, its smooth snowfields and hard-edged rock-faces touched at this moment with soft rose-colour by the last rays of the departing sun, all marvellously sharp against the clear, pale, transparent blue of the sky.

According to our usual way of looking at it, everything that you are seeing has, apart from small changes, been there for thousands of years before you. After a while—not long—you will no longer exist, and the woods and rocks and sky will continue, unchanged, for thousands of years after you.

What is it that has called you so suddenly out of nothingness to enjoy for a brief while a spectacle which remains quite indifferent to you? The conditions for your existence are almost as old as the rocks. For thousands of years men have striven and suffered and begotten and women have brought forth in pain. A hundred years ago, perhaps, another man sat on this spot; like you he gazed with awe and yearning in his heart at the dying light on the glaciers. Like you he was begotten of man and born of woman. He felt pain and brief joy as you do.

---

* E. Schroedinger, *My View of the World*, Cambridge University Press, 1960, pp. 20-22.

Was he someone else? Was it not you yourself? What is this Self of yours? What was the necessary condition for making the thing conceived this time into *you*, just *you* and not someone else? What clearly intelligible *scientific* meaning can this 'someone else' really have? If she who is now your mother had cohabited with someone else and had a son by him, and your father had done likewise, would *you* have come to be? Or where you living in them, and in your father's father…thousands of years ago? And even if this is so, why are you not your brother, why is your brother not you, why are you not one of your distant cousins? What justifies you in obstinately discovering this difference — the difference between you and someone else — when objectively what is there is *the same*?

Looking and thinking in that manner you may suddenly come to see, in a flash, the profound rightness of the basic conviction in Vedanta: it is not possible that this unity of knowledge, feeling and choice which you call *your own* should have sprung into being from nothingness at a given moment not so long ago; rather this knowledge, feeling and choice are essentially eternal and unchangeable and numerically *one* in all men, nay in all sensitive beings. But not in *this* sense — that *you* are a part, a piece, of an eternal, infinite being, an aspect or modification of it, as in Spinoza's pantheism. For we should then have the same baffling question: which part, which aspect are *you*? what, objectively, differentiates it from the others? No, but, inconceivable as it seems to ordinary reason, you — and all other conscious beings as such — are all in all. Hence this life of yours which you are living is not merely a piece of the entire existence, but is in a certain sense the *whole*; only this whole is not so constituted that it can be surveyed in one single glance. This, as we know, is what the Brahmins express in that sacred, mystic formula which is yet really so simple and so clear: *Tat tvam asi*, this is you. Or, again, in such words as 'I am in the east and in the west, I am below and above, *I am this whole world*'.

Thus you can throw yourself flat on the ground, stretched out upon Mother Earth, with the certain conviction that you are one with her and she with you. You are as firmly established, as invulnerable as she, indeed a thousand times firmer and more invulnerable. As surely as she will engulf you tomorrow, so surely will she bring you forth anew to new striving and suffering. And not merely 'some day': now, today, everyday she is bringing you forth, not once but thousands upon thousands of times, just as every day she engulfs you a thousand times over. For eternally and always there is only *now*, one and the same now; the present is the only thing that has no end.

It is the vision of this truth (of which the individual is seldom conscious in his actions) which underlies all morally valuable activity. It brings a man of nobility not only to risk his life for an end which he recognises or believes to be good but — in rare cases — to lay it down in full serenity, even when there is no prospect of saving his own person. It guides the hand of the well-doer — this perhaps even more rarely — when, without hope of future reward, he gives to relieve a stranger's suffering what he cannot spare without suffering himself.

8

Atom Bombs: What do They Imply?*

"Here then is the problem which we present to you, stark and dreadful and inescapable: Shall we put an end to the human race: Or shall mankind renounce war? People will not face this alternative because it is so difficult to abolish war...."

"There lies before us, if we choose, continual progress in happiness, knowledge and wisdom. Shall we, instead, choose death because we cannot forget our quarrels? We appeal, as human beings, to human beings: Remember you humanity, and forget the rest. If you can do so, the way lies open to a new paradise; if you cannot, there lies before you the risk of universal death."

—*Albert Einstein***

The range of destruction of nuclear weapons, which are stocked in large numbers by quite a few nations around the world, is truly colossal. Compared to conventional weapons, the devastation caused by nuclear weapons is extremely difficult to appreciate and assess. Think of a 20 megaton bomb. It releases energy which is of the same order as that of a large earthquake or a hurricane: Its energy is equal to 2 per cent of the total annual output of electrical energy in the world. If this

---

* Based on the concluding chapter of *'Nuclear Explosions and Their Effects'*, The Publication Division, Governnment of India, 1958.

** Extract from a statement issued in July 1955 under the signatures of Albert Einsetin, Percy W. Bridgman, Leopold Infeld, Herman J. Muller, Cecil F. Powell, Joseph Rotblat, Bertrand Russell, Hideki Yukawsa and Jean Frederic Joliot-Curie. [*Science*, 122, 189 (1955)].

bomb were to be made from conventional explosives, the mere cost of the explosives would be roughly thousand million pounds sterling. In terms of destructive power a nuclear weapon is the cheapest thing the world has ever seen — cheaper than conventional weapons by a factor of hundreds, if not thousands. The target that matches this weapon is a huge city: One single weapon by its blast effect alone would be good enough to destroy completely any metropolis. By sheer logic of the situation, megatons bombs and cities cannot co-exist for a long time. In all history the size of political units has, to a large extent, been influenced by the striking power and range of the weapons of destruction. The range of destruction of the nuclear weapons is such that inevitably, as Einstein put it, it must be one world or none. All seem to be agreed that war with nuclear weapons will not end in victors and vanquished, but it can only end in the end of civilisation itself.

We now come to nuclear test explosions which have been and are still being conducted to test new principles and techniques of nuclear weapons. In connection with these explosions there are two points which are extremely important:

(*i*) the internal hazard resulting from ingestion (entry into and absorption in the body) of radioactive substances contained in the fallout from test explosions, the most serious component being radiostrontium,

(*ii*) the genetic hazard from exposure of the entire world population to ionizing radiation from global fallout.

All are agreed that the test explosions do cause harmful effects. What people are not generally agreed about is the magnitude of the harm resulting from them. This question of the actual scale of harm (resulting from test explosions) has, unfortunately, been mixed up with non-scientific and political issues. The scientific knowledge presently available is not enough to give a reasonably clear-cut answer. The assumptions that are made about the permissible radiation burden — somatic and genetic — that an average individual can carry without untoward effects, generally tend to be too optimistic.

Again, as global fallout is uniform all over the world, it is very likely that the first manifestation of its somatic ill-effects would occur in densely populous communities which have a comparatively low standard of nutrition and health. The same is ture of the genetic hazard also. Here the knowledge of relevant factors is so uncertain that any conclusion as to the permissible level of exposure may be in error by a very big factor (even as large as 100). Further, it is very unlikely that the relevant basic knowledge will be available in the near future. This limitation is inherent in the very nature of the subject. It is extremely important that in the meantime (while we are still ignorant as to the true scale of hazard) the radiation exposure is kept down to the lowest possible value; otherwise irretrievable harm may be done to what is literally the most precious treasure of mankind, the genetic heritage.

While no one with any understanding of problems of nuclear war has argued that a war with nuclear weapons would be anything less than a total disaster, there are some people who argue that tests can continue, because it is not yet firmly established that, on the present scale, they would lead to any substantial increase in the existing somatic and genetic load of mankind. In effect, this means that tests can continue so long as it is not known with *certainty* that they would cause serious harm to man. This is a rather strange line of argument. To argue that tests should stop only if it were definitely established that their continuation would bring *certain* disaster to mankind, is a regrettable commentary on 2,500 years of progress since the Buddha. In fact, there can be no doubt at all that if civilisation is to endure and progress what is now necessary — and desperately so — is that the new knowledge of the atom instead of being mobilised for weapons and war, should be mobilised in the cause of peace and plenty.

It is interesting to recall what Einstein declared in 1951:

"Revolution without the use of violence was the method by which Gandhi brought liberation of India. It is my firm belief that the problem of bringing peace to the world on a supranational basis will be solved only by employing Gandhi's method on a large scale.

"Gandhi, the greatest political genius of our time, indicated the path to be taken. He gave proof of what sacrifice man is capable of once he has discovered the right path. His work on behalf of India's liberation is living testimony to the fact that man's will, sustained by indomitable conviction, is more powerful than material forces that seem insurmountable."

In another context, the doyen of historians, Arnold Toynbee wrote in 1970:

"At this supremely dangerous moment in human history, the only way of salvation for mankind is an Indian way.

"In the Atomic Age the whole human race has a utilitarian motive for following this Indian way. No utilitarian motive could be stronger or more respectable in itself. The survival of the human race is at stake. Yet even the strongest and most respectable utilitarian motive is only a secondary reason for taking Ramakrishna's and Gandhi's and Ashoka's teaching to heart and acting on it. The primary reason is that this teaching is right — and is right because it flows from a true vision of spiritual reality."

9

Education and Character Building*

> "The basic aim of education — education at all levels — is to prepare in the young generation a sense of purposefulness and mission, dedication, confidence in themselves and faith in the country's future. This underscores the vital role and importance of 'moral education' and generating an abiding sense of social responsibility and ethical values as integral elements of education in any society secular or otherwise." (p. 132)

The book under review is part educational history, part prescription and operational strategies, and part advocacy to prepare men of sterling character. The addresses very systematically outline how India can earn itself a place on the high table of global educational system. At the heart of the strategy is putting flesh to the bones of the system. Professor Kothari makes a persuasive case for such a relationship not only because of a convergence of hard nosed interests but also because of the shared values of preparing a civilised citizen.

Gandhi said: University is at the top. A majestic top can only be sustained if there is a sound foundation (*Harijan*: November 2, 1947).

The University education is to be such that it turns out true servants of the people, who would live and die for the

---

* *Collection of Convocation Addresses (1962-1983) Delivered by Prof. D.S. Kothari*, National Institute of Science Communication, CSIR, New Delhi, 2000, pp. xvi + 459.

country's freedom. It must be organically related to the Indian scene. There should be a proper background for new universities and not just a manic for establishing new universities. They should have feeders in the shape of schools and colleges which will impart education through the medium of their respective provincial languages. Some of these ideas of Gandhiji have been very well spelled out and articulated in the lectures.

As far as educationists are concerned Gandhiji said: What we need is educationists with originality, fired with true zeal, who will think out from day to day what they are going to teach their pupils (*Harijan*, February 18, 1939). A reading of the 43 addresses will convince us that he does not only subscribe to Gandhi's opinions but makes a plea that in the absence of such committed teachers university education will remain a futile exercise. A teacher has to become a role model not only to students in particular but to public in general also.

A man without education is like a body without soul. Let us recall what J.S. Mill had said about the Price of Freedom. He made two prescriptions in his essay on Liberty: "No vote, no tax, and no tax, no vote" and adult franchise must be preceded by universal education. May be we would have been better off if we had adopted these principles (see M.K.D. Prasada Rao, Affording the price of freedom, *The Hindustan Times*, July 6, 2003, p. 12). This is the need of the hour in India. Education of the right type advocated in the lectures must be developed to have men of character in all walks of life as is evident in the Lilies-in-the-pond story. Let us say the lilies in a pond double every day, there is only one lily on the first day, and it takes a month for the pond to be covered entirely. So on the 29th day, the pond will be half-full, on the 28th day a quarter full, and on the 27th day only one-eight full. To figure out what the future will be like, look at the rate of change. The message of the book is, we will have to have "political will" to implement the suggestions made in the lectures by Dr. Kothari, who had spent his whole life as a devoted and a dedicated teacher. This is the only way to build the nation of Gandhi's and Kothari's dream.

K.D. Gangrade

10

Atom and Self*

After the American destruction of Hiroshima and Nagasaki, Gandhi feared that the availability of such potent devices posed an ominous warning for the future (Mark Juergensmeyer, Fight with Gandhi, Harper & Row, Publishers, San Francisco, 1984, p. 93).

"So far as I can see," said Gandhi, 'the atomic bomb' had deadened the finest feeling that has sustained mankind for ages" (*Harijan*, July, 1946).

Today, what we are seeing is a mad rush of people after wealth, property, and material goods with a false perception of enjoying peace or happiness of mind. To enjoy peace or happiness we have to establish harmony within. This is the main lesson we can draw from the book under review. The 20 lectures, included in the volume, have forcefully brought out the fact that money can't buy either peace or happiness.

What is the happiest place in the world? According to a recent research led by the London School of Economics, the happiest place in the world is (would you believe?) Bangladesh. Interestingly, the United States came in at 46th place in this World Happiness Survey, with Britain at the 32nd mark. India came fifth. Not bad for a land of a billion people with many different races, creeds, castes and religions. The survey reveals how, in general, happiness is inversely proportional to peaks of economic development. Thus, although the British have twice the amount of money they did have 40 years ago, their

* Editor Ahmed Feroz, *Atom and Self — Collection of Lectures Delivered by D.S. Kothari*, New Delhi, New Age International Publishers, 2002, pp. xi + 379.

perceived quality of life has not improved. In fact, it has decreased, the survey tells us. According to one of the researchers, a financial colossus is seducing people all over the world and not meeting their essential personal needs. So, howsoever, amazing it may seem, some now prefer TV to food. The Gita confirms that one whose happiness is within, who is active and rejoices within, is the perfect man or woman. This is the theme which runs throughout the lectures of Prof. Kothari. Prof. Kothari's outstanding contribution has been unique in the fields of education, science and humanism. His brilliant scholarship is reflected in all his lectures and discourses. He has quoted, Gita and Mahatma Gandhi. His basic advocacy is that Science and spirituality cannot be separated. Survival of human race is dependent on integrating both. This will help to wipe out tears from every eye, as well as poverty, and hunger from the planet Earth.

The book is a 'Wake-up-Call' for all the world leaders to make the world free of wars and violent conflicts. They must substitute word by deeds. They must rise above their selfish interests, narrow-groove of nationalism to consider the whole world as a single family by following Gandhi's theory of "oceanic circles". He emphatically says: "The basis of science is its objectivity. Science is alien to purposes and goals. It admits no arguments which smack of any telenomy... The objectivity of science is secured by excluding from its domain all subjectivity. The root of the present crisis, especially of the (western) man, lies in strongly conceiving that what cannot be described by science is necessarily contradictory to science. It is a misplaced case of domination of western mind by Aristotlean logic".

What is important and significant is that we must recognise that 'reality' has not one facet but many. Science is one facet. The different aspects of reality are complementary to one another and not contradictory. This approach is characteristic of Vedantic thought. To disregard the complementarity of scientific and ethical truths, the complementarity of matter and mind, of body and soul can lead only to de-personalisation and dehumanisation of life. The highest type of faith is in science and in man. This is a moral quality. Most significant lesson we can learn from the marvellous development in atomic physics in our century is not to be misled by apparsent contradictions but try to understand the complementarities underlying them. To pursue truth in all its varied aspects, of which ethical is doubtlessly the most important cause, with zest, courage and dedication to the best of one's ability and strength is man's highest duty and obligation. That is the greatest lesson science holds for us. This is also the greatest need of the hour.

In nature, harmony is the normal rule and conflict an exception. Members of the same species never kill one another. Their fights are either sport or ritual. There are few species which deviate from the rule. And the greatest exception is the human species (which calls itself Homo Sapiens). Homo sapiens torture and murder one another in war and peace with wantonness and brutality that has no parallel in nature. No doubt science deals with 'is' and religion with 'ought'. But both are not unrelated. It may not be wrong to say that the future of civilisation depends on the degree to which we can balance the forces of science and religion.

In the atomic age for a world of more than 100 sovereign states, differing more than thousand folds in population and resources, there can be no power and security — and indeed no survival except on the basis of science and *Ahimsa* (non-violence). There is no other way to combat the terrifically rising spiral of Greed, Hatred, Delusion (GHD) and novel forms of political, economic and social exploitation, both within and between nations.

Prof. Deepak Nayyar, Vice-Chancellor, University of Delhi, in his foreword says. "Prof. Kothari draws in his lectures upon his teaching and understanding of quantum physics and Indian philosophy to provide a synthesis of modern science and the Indian intellectual tradition... He was always concerned with the use to which science is put in the contest of society." It would not be an exaggeration to say that the principle underlying Einstein's equation, the basis of relativity, and space-time character of the universe is the same as perceived by the old

Indian Rishis in their advanced stage of spiritual consciousness. In their state of higher consciousness, they realised that the ultimate constituent of the universe, energy and mass, particle and wave—were but different aspects of the same basic process, the same oneness which pervaded the entire universe. The vast knowledge of today cannot transcend the buddhi of the rishis, and science, in its most advanced stage, is closer to Vedanta than ever before. This neglected dimension has been very systematically and analytically dealt with by Prof. Kothari.

Prof. Kothari had a keen eye for details. For readers who feel they are swimming in various speeches and want a single source that bring all the material together, this readable volume has done that exceedingly well.

The scholars, researchers and others would very badly miss the reference index in the volume. This would have enhanced the value of the book considerably.

—K.D. Gangrade

11

Knowledge and Wisdom*

Heritage and Legacy

Shakespeare had said: "There are three types of great men, those who are born great, those on whom greatness is imposed, and third those who achieve greatness." Prof. Daulat Singh Kothari belonged to the last category.

Kothari was born on July 1906. His father died at the early age of 38 years during the plague epidemic of 1918. His mother had to raise young four boys in the face of great economic difficulties. She bravely faced the situation and never lost hope. She by her own personal example taught her children hard work and compassion. She was a highly devout and dedicated mother and adhered to the principles and philosophy of Jain religion. She was a great source of inspiration and strength to all her children and in shaping their destinies. All the four achieved distinction in their respective fields.

Napolean Bonaparte had aptly said; "Give me good mothers and I would produce a great nation". Howard Johnson gave the meaning of the word mother as fellows; 'M' is for the million things she gave me, 'O' means only that she is growing old; 'T' is for the tears she shed to save me; 'H' is for the heart of purest gold; 'E' is for the eyes with love-light shining; 'R' means right, and right she will always be. Put them all together,

---

* Editor Feroz Ahmed, *Knowledge and Wisdom, Collection of Lectures and Addresses delivered by D.S. Kothari*, New Age International (P) Limited Publishers, New Delhi, 2003, pp. xvi+349.

they spell 'Mother'. A word that means the world to me." Abraham Lincoln said; "I remember my mothers' prayers and they have always followed me. They have clung to me all my life". George Washington said; "All that I am, I owe to my mother". (See Sacred Space, *Times of India*, May 10, 2003, New Delhi, p. 16 and also May 11, 2003, p. 19.) She is an Epic to me of Everlasting Love (for details see Tapan Chatterjee, *Ibid.*). A mother's blessing is an immense source of strength. Mahatma Gandhi said, All that I am, I owe to my mother and father.

Fortunately, the Kothari Family has carried forward the legacy and not remained satisfied with the past laurels. I have been a close witness to rise of four generations, especially of "Prof. Kothari's Family". This is despite the fact that about 90 per cent of the present population of India was born after 1947. Of these 90 per cent, the majority belong to the post-Emergency generation — those who are 30 years of age or younger. Trained to recognise a whole minutiae of distinctions originating in caste, class, religion, gender and ethnicity, India's intellectual community is yet to wake up to significance of age. The past can be an exemplar and not a burden. (see, *The Times of India*, Many Young Indians, May 10, 2003, New Delhi, p. 16).

In my study of "conflict of generations" I have found the first generation creates wealth in terms of moral values and ideals, the second preserves them, the third becomes easy going and the fourth wasting. In present day India, we have entered easy going stage. We are not yet into wasting, which means we are programming stagnation. This is neither conducive for individual growth nor for nation-building. The writings of Prof. D.S. Kothari may help us to come out of this morass. Prof. Kothari fits into the definition given by Isaiah Berlin; the great British thinker who had defined a great man as, "to call some one a great man is to claim that he has internationally taken a large step— one far beyond the normal capacities of men — in satisfying or materially affecting central human interests." President A.P.J. Abdul Kalam says, "Learning gives creativity. Creativity leads to thinking. Thinking provides knowledge. Knowledge makes you great." Dr. Kothari had already internalised all these four points.

Dr. Deepak Nayyar, Vice-Chancellor, University of Delhi in his foreward writes that "Dr. Kothari was a visionary as a scientist and educationist..."

The Kothari Commission Report on Education was very well received and was highly appreciated by all the parties concerned. Dr. L.M. Singhvi's comments on the report are worth quoting. He said, "The Kothari Commission Report, like Dr. Kothari himself, was profound without being ponderous, idealistic without being impractical, fundamental without being fanatical."

Prof. A R. Kidwai, former Chairperson of Union Public Service Commission and now Member of Parliament in his highly illuminating Introduction to the book deals with the unique personality of Kothari. He says: "Prof. Kothari was a multi-faced personality. He was an outstanding teacher, a great educationist, a renowned physicist and a highly successful organizer. But above all what struck me (Kidwai) most was that he was an original thinker and a great human being. He was clear, precise and logically presented his views on a wide gamut of subjects ranging from science and education to ethics, philosophy and religion."

He was of the firm opinion that education should be considered as the most powerful instrument for social transformation and for increasing productivity. In this connection he gave a telling example of Japan which achieved nearly 10 per cent of its GNP economic growth in the post-second world war period. This was possible in a generation due to special attention given to technical and general education. He, therefore, believed and advocated that top priority in India must be given to free and compulsory primary education of four to five years duration. He was of the firm view that Education without vision, devoid of ideals, principles and values would be debarring of human dignity and national purposes.

Man wants peace and happiness. The message of the Gita is that the mind is whimsical. It should be kept firmly under the control of the intellect. This will lead to mental peace. Happiness is equal to the number of desires satisfied. Schopenhauer (a German Philosopher) says, if the enjoyment of happiness falls short of the desire for happiness, we say that the man is to that extent unhappy. If this ratio is to be explained mathematically we have to divide the enjoyment of happiness by the desire of happiness and show it in the form of a fraction thus:

$$\frac{\text{Enjoyment of Happiness}}{\text{Desire for Happiness}}$$

But this is just a queer fraction that its denominator, namely the desire for happiness, is always increasing in a greater measure than its numerator, namely the enjoyment of happiness. So that, if this fraction is the beginning 1/2, it becomes later 3/10, that is to say, if the numerator increases three times, the denominator increases five times, and the fraction becomes more and more incomplete. Thus it is futile to entertain the hope of a man becoming fully happy.

Many of us go through life trying to increase, rather than reduce our 'wants' to attain contentment. But the secret lies in the denominator, the number of desires entertained. The smaller that is, the happier you are. And if it is down to zero, you have infinite happiness. Forget the numerator, focus on the denominator. He knows peace who has forgotten desires. (see Jaya Row's discourse on Bhagvad Gita, *The Hindustan Times*, April 11, 2003, New Delhi, p. 17). Indian culture teaches us to be content in all situations.

In an age of Science and Technology we need not only transmission and advancement of knowledge but also imparting a sense of commitment and identification with the community. Science is universal and global, and there can be only a global civilisation. Science encourages cooperation rather than competition. It's roots lie deep in man's highest aspiration and his noblest motivation, more spiritual than material. Prof. Kothari was more spiritual than religious. Whatever the positions he had occupied he remained first and foremost an Educationist.

Knowledge and Wisdom

The title of the book has been wisely kept as Knowledge and Wisdom. Omar Bradley has aptly said: "The world has achieved brilliance without wisdom, power without conscience. Our is a world of nuclear giants and ethical infants." The future of an individual, an individual family, society or nation depends on the health of its conscience. Are we making enough efforts to save our generation as well as coming generations from moral degradation? Similar views have been forcefully expressed by poet T.S. Eliot; "Where is the Wisdom we have lost in Knowledge, where is the Knowledge we have lost in information." Wisdom means unity of Knowledge. It is a discriminating selection and integration of relevant scientific findings. It is the organisation of such knowledge in relation to clearly delineated values. It places human dignity and destiny central in the life process of man.

Wisdom (*Buddhi*) is often mistaken for cleverness. This is not correct. *Buddhi* is essentially the combination of *Shradha* (Earnestness) and *Sathyam* (Truth). *Shradha* is the product of yearning and steadfastness. The aspect implies a proper judgment and perspective, with Truth as the central focus. Cleverness is associated exclusively with worldly skills. *Buddhi*, on the other hand, is spiritual in nature and close to the *Atma*. Thus, one must never confuse a wise person (*Buddhiman*) with a clever person. It is the height of ignorance to equate wisdom (*Buddhi*) with cleverness. The latter is associated with the senses and is thus intimately related to the phenomenal world. It promotes ego, and as long as ego dominates you can not understand anything about self. A clever person would never be able to achieve self-realisation. Only a wise person can. (See Bhagwan Sri Satya Sai Baba, The difference between Cleverness & Wisdom, *The Times of India*, April 4, 2003, New Delhi; p. 2).

When God asked King Solomon if he would want wealth, long life or victory over enemies as a gift from him? Solomon rejected all those and asked God to give him Wisdom to do justice to his people. Similarly, in the Bible wisdom is preferred to gold or silver. The criteria for true knowledge is when our knowledge brings about an humanizing effect in society, when it lets us feel the pain of those deprived of the basic amenities and necessities of life. In such a case I can say without any hesitation that the 21 lectures included in the book are an outstanding contribution to Education and Defence Science.

Prof. Feroz Ahmed, the editor of the lectures and addresses, has cautioned us that we may find some repetition and overlap of material in some lectures. He has not deleted those portions from the lectures in the interest of flow of communication and the audience to which they were addressed. The figures in the text are in the context and period to which they refer.

It is hoped that the material contained in the book would inspire policy makers, educationists, teachers, students and scientists to pay serious attention to missing links and gaps identified by him. It should not allow you to fall in to the illusory trap of a clever 'tailor' who had put up two hoardings: Left hoarding said: "God has created you man", Right one was: "We make you Gentleman". The process has to be to turn information into knowledge and knowledge into wisdom. This will be a real education of man-making. The book has two parts — Education and Defence. Each part along with their respective chapters would be discussed in the following pages.

Part I: Education

This part consists of fourteen lectures. These lectures could have been put under some clusters pertaining to specific themes such as; I. Education and Building of Character and Values; II. Education and the Universities; III. Some other Aspects of Education; and IV. Importance of Medium of instructions. I shall not like to follow the system of chapterisation of the book for the review. I shall follow the clusters approach of chapters as suggested above.

The continuance of widespread violence and unrest throughout the world shows a general decadence of higher moral and ethical values. The lack of fellow-feeling, trust, faith and concerns, superseding personal and group loyalties, is suggestive of the fact that tried and tested path of tolerance, justice, morality, and trusteeship advocated by leaders of yester years, specially Gandhi, Albert Einstein, and others, has been forsaken, particularly by most leaders and people in general. Gandhi had assumed that once people are awakened through Education, they would become a revolutionary force. They would explode if their minimum needs and expectations are not satisfied. The income-gap between the fifth of the World's people living in the richest countries and the fifth in the poorest countries has been widening. It is now 74 to 1, up from 60 to 1 in 1990 and 30 to 1 in 1960. Careful systematic considerations suggest that in order to come out of the present malaise the most important remedy lies in adapting to or adopting the Gandhian system of education with emphasis on three Hs:— Head, Heart and Hand and not three Rs:—Reading, Writing and Arithmetic. This will help towards building of character and moral values, particularly in students and public in general. "Character is Destiny" is the thread running through all the lectures. Let me now take-up clusters of lectures for detailed comments. The figures in the bracket refer to scheme of chapterisations in the book.

Character Building

I. (12) Education and Building of Character
(13) Education and Values

The First address was delivered on the occasion of Golden Jubilee Function of the Faculty of Education, Jamia Millia Islamia, New Delhi, 1988. He stressed that in the Atomic age it is apparent and beyond doubt that the survival of mankind depends on effectively linking education with courage and determination and building character. He reminded the audience that for Mahatma Gandhi *"true education meant building of character"*. That is not possible without including the values of Truth and *Ahimsa* (Love). The whole profession of education should learn some lessons from our great teachers of the past.

It will be educative to learn about the experimental school founded by Gandhi at the Tolstoy Farm in South Africa (1910-

11). "It is possible for a teacher situated miles away to affect the spirit of the pupils by his way of living. It would be idle for me, if I were a liar, to teach boys to tell the truth. A cowardly teacher would never succeed in making his boys valiant, and a stranger to self-restraint. I saw, therefore, that I must be an iternal object lesson to the boys and girls living with me. They thus became my teachers, and I learnt from them that I must be good and live straight, if only for their sakes. I must say that the increasing discipline and restraint imposed on myself at Tolstoy Farms was mostly due to those wards of mine."

The "message" of the teacher to the students is not merely to impart knowledge—content of books which is largely information fast going out of date. But more than that it should be inspiration, by his or her own example, towards the process of character building and the use of knowledge for welfare of the community. The total message to the students, and the community, is the total life of the teacher.

There are four types of teachers. The first is a mediocre or average who only tells; the second is a good teacher who explains; the third is a superior teacher who demonstrates; and the fourth is a great teacher who inspires. Prof. Kothari belonged to the last category. But on the whole there is a dearth of such teachers these days.

Mankind is at cross roads. One path leads to despair and annihilation, the other to immense possibilities of boundless advancement and enrichment-material, cultural and moral-spiritual. All men are born equal and are brothers. It is a supreme moral truth. Man has no future without *Ahimsa* and Science. Science opens up new possibilities of moral experiments, and of insight into reality and ourselves as never before. The role of education lies in promoting a sense of moral commitment.

The second essay on School Education of India, Present Status and Future Needs (1986) says that education is the most powerful instrument for national development, welfare and security of human society. But this instrument must be wisely used, for it is such a potent instrument that if wrongly used it can do great and lasting harm.

We need 'Educated Human Beings' and not mere 'Experts'. What is an 'Expert'? The greatest expert may be having all knowledge—but no wisdom. Knowledge without wisdom or ethical moral values degenerates into arrogance and is of little avail to the individual and the community. When Science and Values (*Ahimsa*) go together, they open a door to a world of liberty, justice, prosperity, and joy for all.

Science and technology are exploding, but wisdom is imploding. Knowledge is expanding but the human personality is shrinking. Because of explosion of knowledge with a simultaneous implosion of wisdom we find grave aberrations and imbalances which have brought mankind to the verge of ruin. Greed, Hatred, and Delusion form a rapidly rising spiral the GHD spiral. The military expenditure world wide per minute is more than a million US dollars (Rupees one crore) to fuel the Greed, Hatred and Delusion spiral. More than half of the total number of scientists and engineers work on the development of weapons of mass destruction. But how tragic is the situation when we come to think of the means of promoting self-control and training in self discipline. Where is the salvation? In all probability it lies in good education and good science, that is, science used to human ends. If salvation lies through education how desperately important it is that it be good education. Today's world situation is to no small extent a result of bad education. Education divorced from values, from character building is no education.

The phenomenon of educational crisis is a part of the dynamic world radically changing in the span of the life time of one generation. One reason for the "Chaos" in education is the burgeoing of new opportunities and aspirations for hundreds of millions who had so long been denied all education and were living at a level of real deprivation. Today education is important for survival and progress, and great are the opportunities—individually and collectively to contribute to man's development. Education is 'dead education' unless it has a research component and it has little utility unless it is to some degree related to productivity. Education which does not value and promote excellence is, in the end, a waste of effort and resource. It should be clear to all that excellence in an individual implies a corresponding obligation to serve the community in one's special field; the greater the excellence, the greater the obligation, especially towards the weaker sections of the community. Education must help to bridge the gap between the rich and the poor, otherwise it would be self-defeating, even harmful. Today great science and great poverty and suffering exist side by side. This is because the passion for knowledge has somehow become divorced from passion for the people. Evil is infectious but good is not so. However, light always triumphs over darkness, and truth triumphs over falsehood. In educational institutions there can be no place whatsoever for violence of any kind, in thought, word or dead. *Ahimsa* is both the foundation and fruit of good education.

The object set before educational institutions has to be not only to train people just for degrees and jobs but to produce men of character.

Universities

II. (1) Education and the Universities
(3) Some Aspects of University Education
(4) Science and the Universities
(5) Education and National Development
(6) Universities and National Development
(8) Higher Education and National Development

With the exception of Science and Universities (Lecture No.4) addressed to the 50th session of the Indian Science Congress rest were addressed to various Conferences of Vice-Chancellors.

Education is the most important single factor in achieving rapid economic development and technological progress and in creating a social order founded on the values of freedom, social justice of our times is the terrific growth of knowledge, especially in the field of science and technology. But the disturbing wide-gap between the rates of growth of scientific and non-scientific activities lies at the root of many contemporary problems.

It is apparent that any large scale expansion of higher education almost always leads to some deterioration in the standard of educational attainment. Whereas physical facilities like school buildings, university teaching blocks, laboratories can be build within a few years, it takes many more years to train competent teachers. In the university education, it is of the utmost important to ensure high standards at all levels, and if any thing, it is even more important at the post-graduate and research level. He exhorted the VCs to make good what is not good, and make better what is good. It a task as vital as it is challenging. Of course, there is no royal road, but with faith and hard work, the goal is not too distant.

He has often quoted Jawaharlal Nehru's idea of a university: "University stands for humanism, for tolerance, for reason, for the adventure of ideas and for the search for truth. It stands for the onward march of the human race toward even higher objectives. If the universities discharge their duties adequately, then it is well with the nation and the people."

He has critically examined the role of university as a society of students and teachers dedicated to the pursuit of learning, accumulation of knowledge, its transmission to succeeding generations and exploration of new knowledge. A university combines education and discovery, teaching and research and in this combination lies its peculiar strength. He is firm believer that teaching and research flourish best in combination and they both wither in isolation. Strangely enough, he has defined education in one word, that word is 'Controversy'; where concord arises, learning withers, where conflict rules, education flourishes.

Scientific knowledge and things directly related to science have been growing at an exponential rate. In the contemporary world rich countries are those which are rich in science and poor are those which are poor in science. Prof. Kothari reminds us that Atom and *Ahimsa*, or, to put it differently, man's knowledge of outer space and of that within, are not in balance. It is this imbalance which mankind must seek to redress. India has made many glorious contribution to world culture, and perhaps the most important and profoundest of them all, is the concept and ideal of non-violence sought, expounded and lived by Buddha, Mahavira, and Gandhi in our times, and which millions have striven to follow after them. The greatest contribution of Europe doubtlessly is the *scientific revolution*. If they join together in a symboitic combination they will usher in a new level of purposefulness, prosperity and spiritual insight into the contemporary world.

Man faces the choice of rolling down a nuclear abyss to ruin and annihilation or raising himself to new heights of glory and fulfilment as yet unimagined.

Prof. Kothari advocates that the real strength of science lies in its relentness, vigorous and fearless pursuit of truth. Scientific laboratories which less than a hundred years ago were curiosities and rare, are now studded all over the globe. Science teaching in India first started in the Calcutta Hindu College (which later became the Presidency College). Any discovery made anywhere soon becomes the common property of all. The language of science is a common language, and its achievements the heritage of all — the only truly common heritage. The world of science is an open one, and this has essentially not altered despite certain aberrations it has suffered because of its close connection with the apparatus of war. Now teaching of science and research has spread to almost all the universities in India.

We are spending only 3 to 4 per cent of GNP on education. The Kothari Commission had laid special stress on pursuit of quality and excellence in education at all levels and in all sectors, whether it may be the education of a scholar or of an artist, or of a pure scientists or of a peasant.

Prof. Kothari introduced a number of innovations as UGC Chairperson, such as Centres for Advanced Studies, Department of special assistance, Examination Reforms, Special attention on Girls Education, Financial assistance to teaches to attend national and international seminars and conferences. Special research grants were also made available to encourage excellence in education and to contribute to national integration and development. He was responsible for the creation of posts of Pro-Vice-Chancellors in the universities to assist the Vice-Chancellors. There is not a single item of education which has escaped his keen eye. Other countries have followed suggestions and recommendation of Prof. Kothari Commission to reform their education system.

Everybody should accept his fervent plea that a great university belongs to the entire country, not only to his city, or his State and to a large measures belongs to the international world of learning. The "roots" of an educational system are, as it were both below and above: the roots below spreading into native soil represent universal primary education whereas the roots above, that is the advanced centres, help in gathering nourishment knowing no geographical boundaries. No country whatever its stage of development can afford to stand aside. The "twin home" of research should be universities and industry, with effective cross-connections. That should be the national policy.

Some Aspects of Education

III. (9) Teaching Linked to Needs
(11) Education for Developing Countries in a world in transition
(7) Education Surges
(2) Some Aspects of Secondary Science Education
(10) Crisis in Education

In India in 1968, as we all know, the average national income per person was something like Rs.400 per year. The total expenditure in our country on education and research divided by the total population of country was a paltry sum of Rs.10 per year while for the United States it was Rs.2,000 per person per year. Gandhi said, for him the touch stone for judging the merit of a proposal on an action was the benefit, so ever small, it would bring to the lowliest man in the country.

For education itself there could not be a more noble and meaningful touch stone than that advocated by Gandhi.

In a developing country top priority should be given to effective primary education, free and universal, and to adult-education. A literate working population is absolutely essential to avail of modern science and technology and new development on the horizon, *e.g.* nuclear energy, automation for major improvement in agricultural and industrial productivity. Change is not the same thing as progress. Progress implies great goals—material, cultural and moral.

Over 85 per cent of all students, largely undergraduate, are enrolled in the affiliated colleges, taught by teachers who have little say in deciding the course contents as well as in the conduct of examinations. The result is a serious distortion of education with abnormal emphasis on covering the course. Gandhi wrote in 1947, referring to his scheme of basic education through handicrafts, that it was not dependent on money, and that the running expenses should come from the educational process itself. He said; whatever the criticism may be, I know that the only education is that which is self supporting. Education should not be concerned only with imparting knowledge but also promoting in young people a sense of commitment and dedication.

We must ensure that the new generation studying in the schools, colleges and the universities is taught what is reasonably modern and not fed on what is obsolete. It has been aptly said, what is in print is *ipso facto* out of date. At the stage of school education, specialisation should be avoided as far as possible. A school syllabus or curriculam must be directly related to the competency of the available teachers. A first-class syllabus without first class level books and other essential teaching aids, would in the hands of third-rate teachers result in chaos and confusion.

In the past, things were allowed to muddle through, as it were, and society made no deliberate effort to adjust education to its material, cultural and spiritual needs. The present world is a world of rapid change, a world of science and technology, a world which is in perpetual flux. One has to appreciate this and realize that the knowledge would be about four times more in 30 years time. Therefore, the strategy to solve crisis in education should be flexible, innovative, and non-dogmatic pursuit of its excellence, and relevance must be aim.

The most important factor which Prof. Kothari had wanted all of us and specially educationist to recognise was that the youth of today is far more mature than it was any time before. The reason being that it has far greater opportunity to educate itself. Today's youth is a competent, hyper educated youth, though the channels in which it is directed is not always to its best interest. If violence erupts at the campuses it must be the function of colleges and universities to make an objective and dispassionate study of crowd psychology.

Importance of Language

IV.(14) The problem of Scientific and Technical Terminology in Indian Languages.

As far as the medium of instruction is concerned Prof. Kothari has justifiably argued that the Universities have to function largely on a bilingual basis instead of a monolingual basis, that is the regional language and English. For post-graduate study and research and to serve as a link for inter-communication between universities, and also with the outside world, English is an obvious choice.

The growth and development of a subject, whether belonging to science and technology or otherwise, involves inevitably the evolution of a technical terminology appropriate to it. This is essential for precise thinking and intercommunication to insure that the same words do not mean different things to different people studying the same subject. A large scale popularisation of science can be achieved only if done in the regional language.

Part II: Defence Science and its Organisation

(15) Science and its Organisation for Defence

This paper critically examines importance of science for Defence. It is said, "That a person who practices science for its own sake is like a glutton who eats for the sake of eating." In the present world science is the most potent force conditioning human progress, and its potentialities both in peace and in war. In India in 1949 at the time of delivering address to the First Defence Science Congress, it was mentioned that there was only one scientist for 100,000 of the population. The total expenditure on research stood at one-fiftieth of one per cent of our national income, that is, about one-third of one per cent of central budget.

The success of Defence Science Organisation ultimately depends on the quality and character of the men who constitute it. It is well known and it is true the world over, that scientists generally prefer a university atmosphere of work, more than any thing else. They are, if not averse, at any rate, not overeager for Government service and work in Government establishments where the atmosphere for scientific research is very often primitive. It may be a good lesson from the case he has quoted from America. "One scientist complained that during a trip which he had taken at his employer's instance he had found necessary to travel a distance of thirty miles between two small towns. Upon turning in his expense account he found that he should have travelled by train whereas he actually travelled by bus. Because of this he charged the Government twenty-six cents more for this portion of the trip than he should have done. Admittedly, the scientist should have dropped the matter there and accepted the loss of twenty-six cents. Instead, he started a long correspondence to prove the validity of his actions. In this correspondence a great deal of more than twenty six cents was wasted on postage, paper, secretarial time, and the scientists time in the almost endless interchange of letters. This finally resulted in the scientist leaving government service without his twenty six cents. This seems to be a nonsensical procedure, and one which eventually lost for the Government a competent scientist."

I am myself a witness to a situation in which a scientist travelled by a bus. He was so much engrossed in his ideas and thoughts that he forgot to retain the bus ticket. He was denied the expenses because he was not able to produce the ticket. The finance officer thought that he may have travelled all the way on foot. It required my intervention to clear his dues. The theory of "distrust" is all pervasive. We go to such a length that we, prefer not to "Trust and Honour" a man's word.

A Defence Science Organisation constitutes a sort of bridge linking fundamental science at the one end and development, design and production at the other end. Dr. Kothari, therefore, provided opportunities for discussion and exchange of ideas between scientists working in the defence establishments and those in the universities and research institutions in the country. This was done with the basic objective to get scientists interested in Defence Research.

(16) The Internal Ballistics of a Leaking Gun

The problems arising out of internal ballistic of gun have been very ably demonstrated by the Professor. He has also suggested some of the remedies to deal with the problems.

(17) Defence Science and its Organisation

This echoes the problems that are similar to those already highlighted in chapter 15 of the book. His stress in this chapter is: A scientist (if true to his profession) must always be busy passionately, busy experimenting and theorizing, but even a life time devoted completely and entirely to it is not enough. Thinking of our times, and possibly of all times, what more a luminous example there can be of disinterested and selfless pursuit of truth, and fearlessness in propagating it, than that of Mahatma Gandhi. Rightly viewed his (Gandhi) was a profound and lasting contribution to the process of the scientific tradition taking roots in our soil (He called his Autobiography "My Experiments with Truth").

The main function of the Defence Science Organisation must broadly be to help the integration of scientific and military thought. The work in the Defence Organisation can be classified as: (1) Performance of weapons and equipment, (2) Operational Research; (3) Special Studies *e.g.*; defence food problems; and (4) Preliminary sorting out of problems for detailed study in appropriate establishments.

The rest of the lectures 18. Science and Defence; 19. Physics and Armour Penetration; 20. Nuclear Weapons; and 21. Science and Defence bring effective relationship between science and Defence and *vice versa*.

Prof. Kothari was very much fond of getting participation of all official and people concerned to get new ideas and implement them with their help. He encouraged grass-root joint thinking; that is between scientists and soldiers. This implies a break with the tradition. It demands radical adjustment on the part of all concerned. It implies a free and forthright discussion (free from rhetoric and inventive) of problems but in an atmosphere of mutual regard and confidence.

A scientific man should also be the complete man, "Citizen of the World". He should not only be fit to live, but also fit to live with.

As Prof. Kothari's life and work demonstrate and emphasise that without Education and Science national salvation and advance can neither be achieved nor won. Let me illustrate this from a recent event from Bastar, a district of Chhatisgarh (India). It produces more than 4,000 metric tonnes of amchoor (a product from Mango fruit) per annum in two grades—black and white. Customers prefer white. In research it was found that the amchoor cut with iron knives turned black whereas the amchoor cut with steel knife remained white. A stainless steel knife cost Rs.10 and iron Rs.2. Using iron knives tribals lost Rs.400 lakhs (see K.S. Ram, Small Inputs, Big Changes, *Times of India*, April 15, 2003, New Delhi, p. 12).

Conclusions

Once upon a time, Indians intitutively understood what knowledge was all about. It was more about people and the process of learning than imbibing "facts" and "information". From Vedic times, the oral tradition of knowledge transmission made it essential to keep the individual at the centre of the learning process. In the *gurukul* system, *guru* and *shishya* interacted continuously, and in a holistic manner, with a few artificial barriers separating one's daily life from worklife and "classroom" learning under a tree. Sadly, most of that tradition has been lost, and today's classrooms have less to do with reality and learning than with cramming and drilling in of information. (see R. Jagannathan, Editor's Note, Learning to Learn may be the key to success, *Indian Management*, Vol. 42, Issue 5, May 2003, p. 9)

Prof. Kothari has done the essays on education and defence with attention to meticulous detail, without losing sight of the longer picture. For him they meant a search for the all inclusive self, the constant partition of self awareness by individual and collective ego. The book is a loosely-strung set of essays. However, essays have admirably succeeded in presenting complex philosophical and the ethical values. An exhaustive and comprehensive introduction by the editor was needed to integrate these essays. Let's not shed tears for our education and defence system. And let's see what we can get from the new world order based on Kothari's suggestions and recommendations. There is no doubt that knowledge is power. Only high standard of moral and ethical education can empower people and give them much needed wisdom. Let us not be satisfied with stereotype of reforms in the education system. Let us be bold enough to change the total system. The present system is like a human body with no soul.

The essays offer many examples to illustrate their immense reach how every day choices, together can lead a society from non violence to violence and waste, or in reduction of a higher way of living. They present that life should be considered as a field where actions and desires are sown like seeds, which germinate, grow and yield fruit that eventually scatters more seeds. This vast network of cause and effect is what is meant and developed by Prof. Kothari as a Karmyogi. We must learn to stand firm in situations where we used to crumble, stand lovingly and respectfully where we used to get resentful, hostile, or vindictive. He succinctly tells us that science provides opportunities for action but does not tell us how these opportunities are to be used. It confers knowledge but not wisdom. It is important to point out here that knowledge and compassion or wisdom must always go in direct proportion and not in inverse proportion. E.F. Schumacher while endorsing this view said: "No one is working for peace unless he is working primarily for the restoration of wisdom."

Prof. Kothari in his working life did not mix personal and professional relations. He was a loving teacher and an ideal citizen. He saw the modern world as dehumanizing, a circumstance that called for radical analysis and an active effort for social change through education. He was unabashed visionary. The new society he longed for was egalitarian communities, society to be restructured in accord with what he conceived to be the naturally harmonious disposition of ordinary human beings. Such basic instincts of trust and generosity, however, could fully emerge only with the demise of the dreary and despolic institutions of the day. Like Gandhi, his point of view was that only real transformation of this world into a better one had to begin with an inner change. It had to be conversion of the heart.

The greatest deficiency of the book has been the absence of a detailed introduction of each part, and an index. But for what we have been given we are grateful to the editor and to Prof. D.S. Kothari Centre for Science, Ethics and Education.

—*K.D. Gangrade*

12

Science and Humanism*

Professor D.S. Kothari's life and contributions can be summed up as "Science plus Spirituality." This should be the golden rule of the education system in all countries. If this becomes minus it will fast slide us down in ethical values. The aim of education has to be to unfold potentialities in the child and not to stunt them. Knowledge is important. But many people with only minimal education make a great success of their lives. Their secret is not knowledge, but the ability to work, to find inspiration and inner guidance.

In fact, many of the most successful people in this world have had very little formal education. For example, Thomas Alva Edison was sent home from school as not competent to be taught anything. Albert Einstein's teachers predicted that he would be a failure. Genius and unusual ability never follow the worn traits. Their natural thought is not, "What have others done, to succeed". Instead, it is, "what does this particular situation, as a thing in itself require of me?" They instinctively understand that whereas human knowledge defines already trodden paths, the divine *Spirit* in man creates everything one is never repeating itself. This has been the secret of success of Prof. Kothari in respect of a variety of responsibilities entrusted to him and a number of high positions held by him.

He firmly believed and practiced that conformity, orthodoxy, the party line are out of place in the academic world.

---

* Ahmed Feroz (ed), *Science and Humanism: Collection of Articles, Addresses and Speeches Delivered by D.S. Kothari*, Galgotia Publications Pvt. Ltd., New Delhi, 2004, p. 374.

He was of the view that Science, *Sarvodaya* (Development of all), *Ahimsa* (Nonviolence) make a golden triangle which symbolizes man's destiny and his future.

There is a phenomenal growth of science and in particular the discovery and control of nuclear energy. In the age of atom, there is to be either one world or none — and there is every hope that the choice will be in favour of former. In times ahead role of violence can only be negative and in the end suicidal for man. Violence corrupts the goal, but non-violence makes "good" even better. Lives of individuals and nations are laboratories for the practice of non-violence. Every 'experiment' helps. It is an endless quest.

The transition from a violent to nonviolent society cannot be anything but most arduous, risky and long drawn journey which may take decades and even centuries for completion. But the first step roust be taken here and now, and deliberately. It is man's single good fortune that the 'atom' and Gandhi were synchronized in the time — they need to be synchronized in the hearts of men.

Gandhi was shocked at the use of the atom bomb by the United States of America against Japan; "He described it as the most diabolic use of science." It was only in the latter half of the 20th century that Gandhi's methods came to be invoked across the globe, in Asia, Africa, America, and Europe. But it was soon forgotten by the rulers of America and Britain during the war on Iraq.

We need to make distinction between the knowledge of an event and awareness of its context. Infusing prejudice in the minds of people, which reaps a contentious future, seems totally counter productive. An education system that builds upon a child's first triumphant channeling of positive energies, as a doer will create a society of individuals who have achieved a sense of unity within individuals, who seek interrelatedness not isolation, plurality not conformism. Individuals, who seek to resolve conflict within human parameters and build a nation or commonwealth that grows out of the life breath of communities in the most natural manner is like a bud becoming flower. This has been the main theme and thrust of all lectures and speeches of Prof. Kothari.

Prof. Kothari felt that the strength of a university lies in the fact that it combines Discovery and Education; and Teaching and Research. He was very strong advocate of the view that teaching and research both flourish in combination, and they both wither in isolation. It is misleading to talk of balance between teaching and research.

The human use of Science and Technology is no easy goal. It demands vision, courage and above all faith. The scientific community has a major and primary role. The first imperative is to promote its varied aspects, at national and international levels, and human implications of science and technology.

Modern Science makes it clear and inevitable that in the operation of nature there is no place, no role whatsoever, for the supernatural. The reign of reason and logic is supreme. This is no simple, no obvious conclusion. It was not apparent in the days of Newton, and Akbar, not to think of earlier times. There is a real need for a philosophy of human implications of science. To this India, in the years to come, could and we hope would, make a distinct and enduring contribution. It is to bring about a transition from science and technology at the expense of man, to science and technology for man. From non-humanistic to humanistic technology. This may appear a dream today, but then today's a dream is often the reality of tomorrow. That is the most inspiring, unforgettable lesson of science. Let us remember, in the light of modern knowledge, that a new-born child of any people anywhere is capable of imbibing any culture if exposed to it early enough. Man is one family. Divisions are man-made and their overcoming is in man's own hands. Man should never allow science and technology to be his master.

There is an in-depth understanding of science and Vedanta by Prof. Kothari and other scientists specially Erwin Schroedinger, who received Nobel Prize for his epochal contribution to modern theoretical physics. He writes:

> "the only solution to the unfathomable mind-body paradox, in so far as any is available to us at all, lies in the ancient wisdom of Upanishads." Schroedinger says that

every mind that has ever said or felt "I" is the person (if any) who controls the motions of the atoms; controls the universe according to the Law of Nature. This is the *Vedanta* formula; self = SELF. The formula, self = SELF, is simple as a formula, but how to comprehend it and activate it in one's life. What is the way? Says Sri Aurobindo (in the concluding chapter of the Essays on the *Gita*): "Follow the law of your *Swadharma* and do the action that is demanded by your *Swabhava* whatever it may be. Reject all motives of egoism, all initiations by self-will, all rule of desire, until you can make the complete surrender of all the ways of your being to the Supreme... This is the deepest and most intimate truth of your real, your spiritual existence."

In *Hind Swaraj,* Gandhiji said: "The real Swaraj is self-rule or self-control." In March 1951, Einstein declared:

"Revolution without the use of violence was the method by which Gandhi brought liberation of India. It is my firm belief that problem of bringing peace to the world on a supranational basis will be solved only by employing Gandhi's method on a large scale." Within a span of 40 years, two world wars killed many tens of millions of people. How deep and pervasive are the effects of GHD (Greed, Hatred and Delusion)?

It is man's great good fortune that science, perhaps unexpectedly, is now slowly but steadfastly moving towards a more unified world view which includes both knowledge and value as complementary and mutually reinforcing.

Science, Technology and Productivity (S-T-P) by themselves cannot generate and ensure national development. Prof. Kothari's concern was that we need with S-T-P a real passionate concern for the people, specially the poor and underprivileged. S-T Development has unlimited potential and power. If wisely used, it opens the path to continual progress in knowledge, happiness and wisdom. But used unwisely it can lead only in this Atomic Age to universal suffering and total disaster.

Indian philosophy and modern science share common feature at the level of parallels between isomorphic themes and problems. First the search for unity in theoretical physics began with Albert Einstein. The search for a fundamental theory, Steven Weinberg says, lifts human life above the level of farce. The second similarity concerns the debate on the nature of reality and the ability of our concepts to represent reality. Vedantic and Buddhist schools rejected the *Nyaya* view: the real was expressible. For the Upanishads, the fundamental realm is where words return, unable to reach the mind. Nagarjuna, the Madhyamik Buddhist philosopher, argued that concepts were inadequate to describe reality by exposing the inner contradictions of concepts like motion and rest. It may be worthwhile to recall the debate between Einstein and Niels Bohr, the former maintaining that physics should give a causal, observer-independent account of reality, while the latter believed that microphysics had to be content with a pastiche of concepts for the same physical system. Modern science lacks an adequate account of the mind. The strict separation between mind and matter enforced by Descartes, allowed matter to be viewed as pure mechanism, explicable in causal terms. Major schools in Indian philosophy such as the Advaita Vedanta, *posit* the *atman* as the sole reality and phenomenal reality as *Maya*, neither absolutely true nor absolutely false. Barring the Austrian physicist Erwin Schroedinger, who affirmed his commitment to the Advaita Vedanta in a tract written shortly before his fundamental papers on wave mechanics, few physicists regard a unitary consciousness as the fundamental reality. Buddhist philosophers on the other hand, regarded consciousness as composite of factors. However, the application of quantum theory runs against the Cartesian grain of disenchanting the material world. It unifies East and West, mind and matter.

Prof. Kothari's lectures and addresses were scholarly and brilliantly written. The language was simple and lucid which made layman to understand some of the complicated technical language of science and technology. The lectures were highly stimulating and inspiring. They broke new paths and encouraged young scientists to take teaching and research as their career.

His life's every moment was devoted to serve humanity. His Biographical profiles of a few scientists such as Lord Rutherford of Nelson, Acharya Jagdish Chandra Bose, Prof. H.J. Bhabha, Prof. Satyendra Nath Bose, and Prof. Meghnad Shah are worth reading to get insight into their pioneering research and dedicated service to humanity. Their examples are really worth emulating. Incidentally the year 2004 also marks the centenary year of renowned physicist, Prof. Satyendra Nath Bose. The other writings are informative and give guidelines to revolutionise science curriculum.

The contents of the book have been classified into three parts. The first part deals with Scientific Humanism. The second part is devoted to Complementarity Principle and Indian Philosophical Thoughts. The Third Part has included some other writings of D.S. Kothari: It contains three sections: A. Addresses and Speeches, B. Biographic Profiles and C. Other Writings.

The introduction by Dr. K. Venkatasubramaniam, Member, Planning Commission, gives a panoramic view of Prof. Kothari's achievements and contributions. He concludes that Dr. Kothari is no more with us. But his ideas and thoughts will live for ever." He quotes poet Shelly who wrote in memoriam of Keats:

> "Some live a life
> A few live beyond"

Yes, Dr. D.S. Kothari would. Prof. Deepak Nayyar in his foreword writes that Prof. Kothari was a great scientist and educationist who made enduring and important contribution in the field of science, education and defence organization.

Prof. Feroz Ahmed deserves our congratulations and three cheers for his painstaking stupendous work. Firstly, for bringing out into four volumes works of Prof. Kothari particularly for students, scientists and lay public in general. Secondly, as coordinator of Prof. D.S. Kothari Centre for

Science, Ethics and Education established by University of Delhi; Thirdly, encouraging students and scientists to accept challenges of modern times so that science and technology serve humanity to bring their all-round development.

I am sure and confident that the present volume gives a clear direction to science and technology to serve modern strife-stricken world.

I shall like to give in some details achievements of scientists.

1. Rutherford was one of the greatest experimental geniuses of the world has ever produced. He was also a great fighter for the cause of science with Civil Service Bureaucracy. His attacks were very telling. He was responsible for liberating the Board of Scientific and Industrial Research from bureaucratic control and bringing it to the control of technocracy (scientists and technicians who understand the thing). He belonged to that very small number of supreme investigators like Archimedes, Galileo and Faraday.
2. Acharya Jagdischandra Bose occupies a high, almost unique position in the history of Indian science. His work broadly falls under three periods: from 1894 to 1899, he was concerned with the study of electric waves, between 1899-1900 biophysical field, and beyond 1903 with the study of plant-responses under physical stimuli of various types. For these studies he developed and constructed his own instruments which were remarkable for their originality and extreme sensitivity. He was a great man of science in that period in India. But he was a lone worker — a towering but isolated peak rather than a builder of a school of scientific research. We should remember his memorial words uttered at the end of the lecture at the Royal Institute (London) in January 1897: "The land from which I come did at one time strive to extend human knowledge, but that was centuries ago. It is now the privilege of the West to lead in this work. I would hope, and I am sure I am echoing your

sentiments, that a time may come when the East, too, will take her part in this glorious undertaking and that at no distant time it shall neither be the West or the East, but both East and West, that will work together, each taking her share in extending the boundaries of knowledge and bringing out the manifold blessings that follow in its train." He has left behind nineteen volumes which form a record of the work carried out and directed by him over a period of nearly thirty-seven years.

3. Prof. H.J. Bhabha: He was a leader of science of the highest distinction and Chairman of the Indian Atomic Energy Commission. His vision was to build in the course of time a school of physics comparable to best anywhere and India will not require to look abroad for its experts but will find them readily at hand.
4. Prof. Satyendra Nath Bose: He has a permanent place in the vocabulary in the world of physics. The epoch-making four-page article of Bose on Planck's law and light quanta was published in 1924, in the *Zeitschrift fur physik*. It was communicated by Einstein himself translated from English into German.

   Bose's published work, largely in thermodynamics and relativity, is small in volume but its influence has been extraordinarily far reaching. He was founder of the Bangiya Bijan Parishad (Association for Science in Bengal) and its monthly Journal.
5. Prof. Meghnad: His name would always remain associated with the theory of thermal ionization and its application to the interpretation of stellar spectra. Saha's research in astrophysics and physics extended over a wide range of subjects. He built several laboratories and institutions to encourage young scientists and develop scientific temper in people. He was so popular that he was elected as an independent member of the Indian parliament. He took keen interest in problems of national planning, particularly in relation to science and industry. His

> memory and versality were amazing. He was a man of undaunted spirit, resolute determination, untiring energy and dedication. In his criticism of things and men, Saha was fearless and trenchant, and he was motivated by a deep earnestness and sincerity though often tenaciously held conviction.
>
> The most fundamental discovery on which rests the entire edifice of modern physics or modern science is the Principle of Complementarity.
>
> Niels Bohr, to whom together with Heisenberg, essentially we owe the principle of complementarity, had to choose a Coat of Arms, when he was awarded the highest honour of Denmark by the Danish King. Niels Bohr chose the Latin motto which says "contraries are complemantary."

This is very similar to the basic philosophy of the Upanishads. Sri Aurobindo said that the Upanishads seek an uncompromising reconciliation of the material world and the spiritual world. It is this process which leads to man's spiritual evolution. We cannot realize these goals for which man's great urge is there either on the basis of matter alone or on the basis of spirit alone. It has to be reconciliation of the matter and the spirit, i.e. the reconciliation between the *para* and *apara*.

If we forget the one or ignore the other we will only meet disaster. It is in this sense that one can understand the famous Russel Einstein joint statement issued in 1955 about the nuclear horror that is facing mankind — which can reduce mankind into dust and ashes. The statement says that remember your humanity and forget the rest; if you can do so then there lies a new paradise; if you cannot do so then mankind sooner or later will meet total disaster. So, here again there is complementarity.

If we emphasize our differences and think of ourselves individually, then we are separated from one another. If we think of our spiritual existence, then we immediately realize that we are all one. But in terms of complementarity principle, we immediately realize the unity of mankind. The complemantarity principle should be taught in schools. This principle rather than any other religion will help in moral and spiritual advancement of mankind.

Ultimately the progress of society depends on its willingness and capacity to seek truth and to regard pursuit of truth as its highest duty and obligation. In fact, the roots of scientific endeavours, as of all creative effort, are, in a profound sense essentially spiritual.

As a non-student of science it has added to my knowledge of science and its intricacies. It is simple and academic, poignant, interesting, gives basic and highly useful information. Even the lay persons would find a better understanding of science and technology for the use of society and to build a peaceful world. The appropriate government policies and education can help in wiping out tears of world's poor people.

Let us "hope" that goodness would dawn in man, he would give up the method to resolve conflicts or disputes by means of violence. There is a proverb which says "If man lives in HOPE, happiness and peace will come in his way sooner or later."

Prof. Kothari remained throughout his life a 'teacher' who followed the dictum of Socrates that, "I would like to learn and learn".

In a nutshell his works would help us to imbibe the lesson of renunciation (Aparigraha or non-possession) to attain genuine peace and happiness. The principle of Aparigraha would not allow greed to dominate our thoughts and actions to over accumulate. Let us be optimistic that as science has transformed our outer world, similarly, the inner world too can be transformed with the science of spirituality. Materialism and spiritualism must go together to achieve peace and harmony.

In India 65 per cent of the population lack basic sanitation facilities. We are not utilizing technology to its optimum. When we start doing so we will be able to save a lot of time and energy. A further examination of data tells us that:

(1) As many as two billion people do not have ready access to clean water; (2) 2.4 - 2.9 billion people have no sanitation facilities; (3) 6,000 children die every week from water related diseases; and (4) It takes 1,000 tonnes of water to raise one tonne of grain, but 16,000 tonnes of water to raise one tonne of beef. To meet the entire world's basic needs for clean water and sanitation would cost an estimated additional $9 billion per year well under the $12 billion spent per year on perfumes and $18 billion on pet foods by Europe and North America. The world spends more than 80 times that figure on the military and armaments. The book, therefore, makes a unique plea and to remind everybody if the extreme importance of 'human relationship' for maintaining the environment and increasing development in human societies to achieve cherished goal of bringing Golden period on earth.

—*K.D. Gangrade*

REFERENCES

Kriyananda, Swami, 'Following The Road to Success (Inner Voice)', *The Hindustan Times*, March 11, 2004, New Delhi, p. 7.

Padmanabhava, Chitra, 'Colonising The Child-Education as an Instrument of Prejudice', *The Times of India*, New Delhi, March 11, 2004, New Delhi, p. 16.

Nair, Ranjit, 'Mind-Matter Divide in Science, Philosophy', *The Times of India*, March 10, 2004, New Delhi, p. 18.

Part III

13

Science and Human Progress*

In a historical sense the most conspicuous characteristic of the contemporary world is the large scale and intense cultivation of science, pure and applied. The course of history during the last few centuries has been profoundly influenced — and this to an ever-increasing extent — by discoveries and developments in science and technology. In fact, we have now almost reached a stage when to-day's science largely determines the economic and political events of tomorrow. This is a new situation in man's history, and it is one which barely three hundred years ago even the great pioneers of science could not have foreseen or even imagined. The wealth and security of a country today is intimately dependent on the level and intensity with which science and technology are developed and harnessed by its people.

Again, the overwhelming impact of science on society has for the first time in human history introduced an element of unpredictability and uncertainty not present in earlier times. This arises from the basic fact that in the very nature of things, fundamental discoveries in science are inherently unpredictable. In passing one may mention that the above reference to the unpredictability in history has no relation with the ultimate question of freedom and creativity *versus* necessity and determinism of historical events: Do men direct and control the stream of history or is it that the stream carries men, like floating straw in a river, along a predestined course? This is an unanswered question, but is it a valid question to ask, or is a

---

* Inaugural Address, The National Academy of Science, Allahabad, 16th February, 1963.

pseudo question which we ask because we do not have wisdom enough not to ask it? We do not know.

In the field of science it is well recognised that what is achieved is in direct proportion to the effort we put into it. Science is no magic. Further, there is no upper limit or ceiling to that it can achieve. Again, science is universal. In its approach and achievements, in its methodology as well as content, it cuts across all sectarian, geographical and ideological frontiers. People in practically every land, including our own, have contributed to the advancement of science and to its sustained progress. A fundamental example that immediately comes to one's mind is that all *elementary particles* in nature, be these electrons, protons or what not are either *Fermions* or *Bosons*. These are named after the late Enrico Fermi and Professor Satyen Bose of the University of Calcutta, who about 1924 first studied the relevant quantum statistics.

Science is a collective activity of mankind, and it is this which has led to its extraordinarily rapid, almost exponential growth. The steam of scientific knowledge has been gathering momentum from generation to generation. The total achievement to date in the field of science and technology is indeed remarkable, and we may sometimes wonder with Whitehead that so little knowledge has given us so much power. But even more remarkable is the *pace* or *rate* of scientific progress. Scientific knowledge is doubling itself in some 10-15 year's time. (A rate of 7 per cent per year is equivalent to a doubling period of 10 years.) This doubling period can be estimated in various ways. For instance, the number of scientific journals and periodicals which was about 100 at the beginning of the 19th century is now about 100,000, implying a doubling period of 15 years. If this rate of expansion were maintained, the number would be of order of a million by the year 2000 A.D.

The 'doubling period' denotes the time which it takes for the relevant quantity (number of journals in the preceding example) to double itself. A doubling period of the order of 10-15 years is exhibited by such diverse items as the number of physics abstracts published annually; number of road accidents per year; number of stars catalogued by astronomers; speed of aircraft; production of steel; output of coal; magnification of microscopes; output of electricity; world energy production; and so on.

A common characteristic of the above items is that they are directly linked with science and technology. Thus, the number of scientists in a country, or for the world as a whole, shows a doubling period of 10-15 years, but this is not true in the case of poets, statesmen or saints. The doubling period of poets is about the same as for the total population that is about 50 year. [The doubling period for the Gross National Product (G.N.P.) of the U.S.A. is about 20 years.] Curiously enough, even the number of elementary particles discovered during the last several decades shows a doubling period of 10 years. (I.M. Freeman, *Am. Scientist*, December, 1962). (The number of universities in a country has also probably a doubling period of the same order.) A doubling period of 10 years implies that some 90 per cent of the scientists who have ever lived since the beginning of history are alive today. Obviously such a growth rate could not continue indefinitely. Eventually a saturation would set in when the rate of increase of scientists would be about the same as rate of increase of the total population.

One of the striking effects of scientific research and development has been the increase in the average span of human life. There appears, so far, no noticeable increase in the maximum span, which, it seems, is controlled by genetic factors. The mean span of life, however, has been continually increasing during the last hundred years or so. For example, in the case of the so-called 'Advanced countries' there has been an increase of some 15 years during the present century In fact, the rate of expenditure on research and development in different countries shows a direct relationship not only with the *per capita* national income, but also, as would be expected, with the expectation of life at birth.

In the field of scientific knowledge it is important to appreciate that we are concerned with a cumulative activity, with knowledge growing from generation to generation. In the field of science one cannot omit Pythagoras and do only

Archimedes, omit Newton and do only Einstein; but in other subjects (say, literature) one could omit Kalidasa and do Goethe, omit Sophocles and do Shaw. As human population is growing at a much slower rate than scientific knowledge, it is apparent that the 'scientific capital' per person is much more today than what it was, say, a 100 years ago.

In pre-scientific age 'words' and authority supported by tradition or dogma and not reason have played a dominant role. In the scientific age it is work that takes a supreme place. As its social consequence, feudalism gets replaced by democracy and welfare-state.

There is one feature of science and technology which is specially important, and may be explicitly mentioned. In former times when one country helped another, or was forced to assist another by political pressure or war, the donor country lost what was gained by the recipient country. If it was a transfer of land or other material resource, one country could only gain it at the expense of the other. But in the modern world progress and prosperity depend upon harnessing science and technology, the situation is now completely altered. By imparting scientific knowledge and techniques to a less-developed country, a donor country loses nothing. In fact, it is likely to gain something in the process. It is of some importance to recognise that it is in the nature of an exponential growth rate (with a doubling period much less than the population doubling period) which fortunately makes it *possible* that a relatively advanced country *could,* if it so desired, make a major contribution towards the rapid development of a 'newly developing country', say, by supplying an adequate number of technical men, material resources, etc. to serve as "seeding nuclei" for the operation of the exponential growth-process, without sensibly affecting its own economy or rate of progress. It is not the place to pursue this point further, but it is apparent that the main obstacles to rapid progress are now largely political and psychological: There is no lack of resources.

The present century has witnessed an unparalleled growth in our understanding of atoms and interactions between elementary particles. The new understanding that has been achieved in this field has also a wider epistemological lesson. This is not unexpected, since in dealing with atoms we are concerned with one of the deepest aspects of nature. A fundamental lesson of epistemology with which historians and humanists in their investigations have been long familiar has now recently been forced upon physicists, because of the peculiar behaviour of atomic systems as revealed by experiment. It is well recognised that in dealing with an ancient civilisation or society one should be extremely careful not to seriously distort or mutilate the 'picture' by forcing it into a mould of contemporary concepts and ideas (*e.g.* the concept of a 'country', 'nation', 'democracy' and so on) which, inspite of a superficial (and misleading) resemblance, may be totally alien to the ancient culture under study. In recent years the same epistemological lesson has been high lighted in the study of atomic phenomena. For example, even such simple concepts as position and velocity cannot be extended to an electron without recognising an essential and deep-seated limitation in their applicability to atomic systems. This novel situation in atomic physics which has been particularly stressed and clarified by Niels Bohr under the name of the 'Principle of Complementarity' has some features, as regards attitude and approach, which are likely to be of value to humanists and sociologists in their work, and may be even to seekers of the spirit. This is not the occasion to go into the matter further; but two quotations one from Dirac and the other from the Kena Upanishad, would serve to bring out the point to some extent. Dirac says in the Preface to his epochal book on the Principles of Quantum Mechanics:

> "The methods of progress in theoretical physics have undergone a vast change during the present century. The classical tradition has been to consider the world to be an association of observable objects (particles, fluids, fields, etc.)... and to make assumptions about the mechanism and forces connecting these observable objects, to account for their behaviour in the simplest possible way. It has become increasingly evident in

recent times, however, that nature works on a different plan. Her fundamental laws do not govern the world as it appears in our mental picture in any very direct way, but instead they control a substratum of which we cannot form a mental picture without introducing irrelevancies. The formulation of the laws requires the use of mathematics of transformations. This state of affairs is very satisfactory from a philosophical point of view, as implying an increasing recognition of the part played by the observer in himself introducing the regularities that appear in his observations, and a lack of arbitrariness in the ways of nature, but it makes things less easy for the learner of physics. The new theories, if one looks apart from their mathematical setting, are built up from physical concepts which cannot be explained in terms of things previously known to the student, which cannot even be explained adequately in words at all. Like the fundamental concepts (*e.g.* proximity, identity) which every one must learn on his arrival into the world, the newer concepts of physics can be mastered only by long familiarity with their properties and uses."

The Kena Upanishad opens with the grand and challenging quotation:

> "By whom missioned falls the mind shot to its mark? By whom yoked does the first life-breath move forward on its paths? By whom impelled is this word the men speak. What God set eye and ear to their workings?"
> And it continues
> "There sight attains not, nor speech attains, nor the mind. We know not nor can we discern how one should teach of THAT, for it is other than the known, and it is beyond the unknown; so have we heard from the men of old who have declared THAT to our understanding."
> And further
> "He by whom IT is not thought out, has the thought of

> IT; he by whom IT is thought out, knows IT not. IT is unknown to the discernment of those who discuss IT, by those who seek not to discern of IT, IT is discerned." (Translation by *Sri Aurobindo*)

Everyone knows that nuclear physics, space exploration and micro or molecular biology are the most exciting fields of current scientific research. It has been said, for example, that man has learnt during the last 10 years more about the essential life processes, *e.g.*, nature of genes, protein synthesis and so on, than during all the preceding centuries. As Weinberg (*Science*, 21 July 1961) has recently remarked: "The probability of our synthesising living material from non-living before the end of the century is of the same order as the probability of our making a successful manned round trip to the planets". In both cases the probabilities are high, provided the world is not plunged onto a nuclear war. What our own contribution is likely to be in the things to come, great and small, would depend primarily on the emphasis we place on education and pursuit of knowledge.

Mention of the word 'nuclear physics' brings to the minds of most people the horrid spectre of nuclear weapons. Mankind faces today an unprecedented peril, both in depth and extent, in the shape of the possible misuse, deliberate or accidental, of nuclear knowledge. Indeed, nothing less than civilisation and human survival are at stake. If this simple fact is not as widely apparent and forcefully realised as it ought to be, it is largely because there has not been enough serious and sustained effort to inform us about it. And Professor Le Gros Clark observed in his Presidential Address to the British Association last year (1961): "For, let us not deceive ourselves, the frightening question is now beginning to present itself whether the civilisation which mankind has slowly and laboriously built up over a period of many thousands of years can avoid disastrous dissolution as the result of uncontrollable (or, at any rate, uncontrolled) struggles for political power or economic superiority, and, indeed, whether the human species can avoid at least partial extinction by the misapplication of its own ingenuity."

The present unfortunate and tragic situation is essentially a reflection of the widening gap between the rapidly expanding scientific and technical knowledge on the one hand and 'Political wisdom', statesmanship and ethical values on the other. Science and spirituality or 'atom' and non-violence are not in balance. It is this imbalance which mankind must seek to redress.

14

Science and Man's Future*

World is Science and Technology Based

Perhaps, the most significant characteristic of the contemporary world is that it is science and technology based. And in this there could conceivably be no going back unless civilisation itself suffered a total collapse because of man's folly to deal in a human way — that is, in the true interests of mankind as a whole — with the forces of cosmic dimensions that nuclear energy has placed in men's hands. The world is no longer a place of slow and gradual change. As has been said a graduate is obsolescent on the day of his graduation; a research paper (if a good one) in a subject at the expanding frontiers of science is out of date on the day of its publication; and a (science) teacher, unless always a dedicated student, is almost obsolescent before the end of the probationary period. The pace of change and innovation is indeed terrific.

The growth rate of scientific knowledge is exponential. This is, as one would expect, for more science means more possibilities to apply science as also to advance science further. It is common knowledge that ever since the beginning of the scientific revolution some three centuries ago the doubling period of science and technology has been about 10 to 15 years. A doubling period of 10 years corresponds to a compound growth rate of 7 per cent a year. The total number of scientists and engineers in the world — and within a country which has passed the take-off stage in science and technology — is

* National Academy of Science, Annual Session - 1971, Ujjain, 26th February, 1971.

doubling every 10 to 15 years, on an average. The same applies to the number of scientific journals, to the number of scientific publications, and to things directly linked to science and technology, such as, the output of electricity. It is important to recognise that a growth rate of about 7 per cent a year applies to the total "volume" of science and technology. The growth rate of the number of fundamental scientific discoveries — discoveries which determine the direction and quality of the entire scientific enterprise — is much less. Quantity expands much faster than quality. Fundamental discoveries in science are the creations of exceptionally gifted individuals. Their number is likely to be proportional to the total population, and hence the growth rate of fundamental discoveries may not be very different from the growth rate of the world population.

We do not quite understand why science and technology double every 10-15 years. But such a fantastic growth rate cannot be maintained for too long. Sooner or later, it would lead to saturation.

The positive benefits of science and the overall gains to mankind, material, cultural and spiritual, need no reminding. Science is a powerful dispeller of fear and superstition, of fatalism and passive resignation. By debunking magic and sorcery which aimed to control Nature by cheating or cajoling her, science which controls Nature through understanding, through reason, has raised the relationship between Man and Nature to a new level and given a new insight into it. By providing a framework of objective knowledge of natural laws, ever expanding and deepening as each generation adds to it, science has given man a new outlook and a new horizon. Science is hard work; and a relentless and passionate search for truth. Earnest scientific study and research is deeply satisfying and uplifting for it links, it connects, the individual to mankind's cumulative adventure of the mind — perhaps, the greatest in man's history so far. The individual's small and insignificant effort becomes a part of the whole. Through this connection with the whole the individual shares the vision, hopes and aspirations of some of the greatest thinkers of all times and all lands. And by bringing such an uplifting experience within reach of a large number of people, science has contributed immeasurably to strengthening the commitment of man to free enquiry and to the quest of truth as his highest duty and obligation. But the process is by no means automatic. It needs careful watching and nurturing through education, research and wise counsel. Too much emphasis on technology and material achievements of science (as distinct from the spirit of science) which one sometimes comes across in the so-called 'advanced' countries; or also not in so advanced, can lead to serious imbalance in man's culture and an erosion of the moral foundation of society. Too much preoccupation with means of production and material gains, and too little reflection on values and purpose of life, can in the end lead only to self-defeating activity and self-killing frustration. Even more important than the tangible achievements of science is the spirit of science. Growth of science and technology is not the same thing as strengthening of the spirit of science. To accumulate scientific information (or to engage in research) is not to be equated always to imbibing, and practising, the values which science upholds—integrity, open-mindedness, humility, and above all *the discipline of dissent*.

Bentley Glass in his Presidential Address, *Endless Horizons on Golden Age*, to the 1970 annual meeting of the American Association for the Advancement of Science (*Science*, January 8, 1971) has with great earnestness and perception drawn our attention to the fact that the fast growth rate of science and technology cannot be long sustained. As a consequence of this rapid compound-growth-rate which has been on for three centuries, the total "volume" of science and technology (S-T volume) has become so huge that there is not much room for any large-scale further expansion. According to Bentley Glass, there may be at most a generation or two before progress must cease. And he continues: "Let me suggest, at the risk of graves misunderstanding, that in future histories of the world the decade of the 1960s may be known.........as the time when man, with unbridled lust for power over nature and for a so-called high standard of living measured by the consumption of the products of an industrial civilization, set in motion the final speedy inexorable rush towards the end of progress". Where there lie the endless horizons to seek, for without new horizons to explore. Man cannot survive as "man". As Bently Glass says: "We must, then, seek a change within man himself. As he acquires more fully the power to contend his own genotype and to direct the course of his own evolution, he must produce a Man who can transcend his present nature."

Discovery of a New Spiritual World

Mankind is at a momentous cross-roads in history. In the context of the deep crisis man faces today it was most unfortunate that at the beginning of the scientific-industrial revolution in Europe, the West did not know about the culture and philosophic thought of the East, especially India. It is pertinent to recall in this connection the observations of the great historian of science, George Sarton (1884-1956). I cannot refrain to quote him at some length. Sarton says [*The Appreciation of Ancient and Medieval Science during the Ranaissance* (1450-1600), University of Pennsylvania Press, 1955]: "From 1450 to the end of the eighteenth century, that is, throughout the Renaissance and two centuries beyond it, civilisation was largely understood in the sense of Western civilisation, and humanism meant the knowledge of classical antiquities. The Bible, represented by the Vulgate, was an essential part of Latin culture. A new Oriental renaissance occurred only by the end of the eighteenth century when Anquetil-Duperron and Sir William Jones discovered Zend and Sanskrit writings and the complicated pattern of Indic cultures. This introduced a new kind of humanism, more catholic than the Renaissance humanism. Their discovery of a new spiritual world was infinitely more important than the discovery of a new material world by Columbus, Vasco da Gama, Magellan, *E tutti quanti*, but it attracted less attention, and to this day and great majority of the so-called humanists (meaning the teachers of Latin and Greek) are still on the Renaissance level or below... After the Renaissance, the West was fully equipped to continue and complete its conquest of the material world. This implied colonial expansion and the subjection of Eastern peoples to Western needs and greed. The Western nations did not simply exploit and enslave their Eastern Brothers; they did much worse, they failed to appreciate their spiritual heritage and tried to deprive them of it; it was not enough for them to conquer their material goods, they wanted to conquer their very souls. We are today paying the cost of their greed and of their stupidity...

"Ours is a golden age of science, which is fine, but it is also a golden age of technology, business, management, an age of over-organisation and dehumanisation, and that is ominous and degrading... It would suffice to admit that material profits are not as desirable as many good people have been led to believe, and that there is infinitely more virtue and glory in creating beauty, justice, happiness, than in creating wealth. Will the leaders understand that? I am afraid not. Fortunately, whatever their greed for power and wealth may be there will always be room for artists, philosophers, men of science, historians, humanists, if these be satisfied, as they should, to live in a bare competency or better still in blessed poverty".

These are great and inspiring words.

The progress of science has been phenomenal. On the other hand, man's understanding of himself has been dismally slow. Man has gone very far beyond all expectations, with what started with Thales and Greece, but hardly any progress is noticeable along the path lighted by the Buddha. The study of the external World (the study of matter) has turned out to be far easier than the study of man's inner world. As it has turned out, it is infinitely easier to understand the atom, the star and the galaxy, than to understand the "I". At one time man faced Nature and his survival depended on his control of nature. But now the situation is totally different. Man's survival in the age of the atom and the population explosion depends crucially on man's understanding of himself. *Man now faces himself.*

Subject-Matter of Science

What is the subject-matter of natural science? Does science

encompass everything, if not in fact at least in principle? Or is there something, some area, some aspect of experience, which is totally outside natural science? A well-known answer (?) is that the "I" is outside science. In the very nature of things the 'I' that is consciousness and mind cannot be a subject-matter of science: why?

The physical sciences deal with *matter and energy, space and time*. Matter and energy are in principle inter-convertible as Einstein predicted as a direct consequence of the theory of relativity. The relation ($e = mc^2$) underlies all interaction between matter and energy, and is particularly vividly demonstrated in nuclear phenomena. (e is energy, m is mass, at c is the velocity of light in empty space). The relation ($e = mc^2$) is in conformity with conservation of energy, because the velocity of light is a universal constant. The requirement that the velocity of light is independent of the motion of the source of light or the observer necessitated a complete revision of our ideas about space and time. It was a basic postulate of Einstein's theory of relativity which joined (fused) together the separate concepts of space and time into a more abstract and extremely fruitful concept of the four-dimensional *space-time*.

Physical science deals with properties and entities which are measurable. Every measurement is ultimately a matter of observing "pointer-readings", that is, coincidences of two events in space-time *e.g.* the coincidence at some moment of time of the pointer-end with some mark on a scale. Measurements in science are not done at random. An *experiment* is always guided by some theory and is designed to test it. If the result of the experiment disagrees with theory, it is a challenge to revise, or even to discard, the theory. A disagreement between experiment and theory is therefore much more interesting than an agreement — it is this which lends onward momentum to science. A theory is an integrated framework of physical and mathematical concepts (postulates). If a well-established theory permits a simple mathematical formulation, the latter is sometimes referred to as a "law of nature".

The results of all (honest, accurate) measurements are

eventually incorporated in the conceptual framework of science. The "language" of the physical sciences, apart from mathematical concepts, is space and time, matter and energy. Anything which is not describable in this language is outside the physical sciences. There is no exception to this, and there can be none.

We have spoken of the physical sciences. What about biological or life sciences? It has been an achievement of the greatest significance for experimental science in the last hundred years or so to demonstrate that all measurable properties of *living* things (that is, everything except consciousness and mind) can be described in terms of chemistry and physics. The chemistry of, and within, a living cell, not to speak of multi-cellular organism, is extraordinarily complex in comparison to chemical reactions in test-tubes. But all the same the difference is one of degree of complexity and not one of principle. The chemical and physical laws are *exactly the same* whether we deal with animate or with inanimate things. There is no difference whatsoever. And current advances in molecular biology and biochemistry are making accessible to "test-tubes" more and more of the reactions occurring within living cells — for instance Khorana's epochal work on the chemistry of genes. Recall J.D. Bernal's definition of life: "Life is a partial, continuous, progressive, multiform and conditionally inter-active, self-realisation of the potentialities of atomic electron states".

The living body is a machine, *albeit* an unbelievably complex one, but a machine all the same. The "machine" includes of course the brain. What is excluded, and what cannot be a part of the machine, is *consciousness*. But is it really so?

Brain and Mind

Brain and mind are always found together, so far as our experience goes. And if the brain is a machine [a very special kind of super (digital) computer], how can the mind escape to be so. The brain and mind are inextricably bound together. The mind is influenced by the physical and chemical state of the brain. Otherwise, among other things there would be no market for tobacco, alcohol, and tranquillisers. Reciprocally, if the mind did not influence, control the brain, what value the brain (and so the body) would have for me and you: Nothing. All of a man's life and activity, all his pursuits — physical, cultural and spiritual — are an expression of the interaction and coupling between the brain and the mind, or, to put it more generally, as the same should apply even to the lowest animals, between matter and mind. The distinction that Descartes made in this respect between man and animals was pre-Darwinian, and incorrect. Yet of this interaction, we do not have the faintest understanding, not even the faintest clue.

The brain is a seat of intense chemical and electrical activity, of myriads of shifting patterns of electric currents. The mind is sensations, perceptions, feelings and thoughts. That is how it manifests itself to the "I" to whom it belongs. But how can one pattern of electric pulses give rise to sensation of pleasure, another of pain, one a sensation of green colour and another of rose smell? All this is a mystery, nay, more than a mystery.

Note that an individual sensation is not communicable. It is a personal experience impossible to communicate to another. What is communicable, and therefore basis of objective knowledge, is a comparison between two (or more) similar sensations. For instance, there is no sense whatsoever in asking the question whether the "green" sensation I have of the yonder *Neem* tree is the same as yours. But we can compare and communicate to one another whether two objects have the same colour or not.

How can physical and chemical changes in the brain give rise to sensations and perceptions, that is, give rise to something which is totally indescribable in terms of physics and chemistry. That there is a unique correspondence between states of the brain and states of the mind seems beyond question. Some of the great philosophers of the past drew attention to this much before developments in science made possible any serious investigation of the brain. The parallelism between the states of the mind and states of the brain is referred to as the principle of psycho-physical parallelism. There is a "parallelism" between the states of the brain and of the mind, but how this parallelism comes about; there is utter ignorance.

So immediate to everyone of us is the problem of mind-matter interaction, and yet it is so utterly intractable and tantalizing that professional scientists tended to ignore it completely. Professional scientists unlike professional philosophers, spend their time and energy on 'solvable problems' and not on 'unsolvable ones' how so interesting and important these may appear to be. P.B. Medawar, as we know, has called science 'the art of the soluble'. The trend to ignore the mind-matter problem was also reinforced by the fantastic progress of science and technology beginning with the later half of the nineteenth century. Also, because of its long history and fame, the problem has not been without its attraction for crazy people, not to speak of charlatons, aspiring to quick effortless fame. This can become a deterrent to scientists with serious interest in the problem.

The thing is now somewhat changing; the change is more noticeable among physicists than biologists. Partly, this has been encouraged by the epoch-making developments in atomic physics, Niels Bohr's principle of complementarity immediately comes to mind. Partly, the disenchantment with technology, more vocal than substantial, leads to a feeling of inadequacy as regards science. It is this growing current interest in the matter-mind problem that has made me venture to seek your indulgence to speak about a subject so patently beyond my competency. [For instance, E. Schroedinger, *Mind and Matter*; E.P. Wigner, *Symmetries and Reflections*, Bryce S. DeWitt, *Physics Today*, 23 (Sept. 1970); L.N. Cooper and D.Van Vechten, Amer. J. Phys. 37, 1212(1969). The last paper is a good example of confusion between brain and mind.]

It was the usual thing before modern science demolished the walls between the inanimate and the living, to place life and mind (soul) together and matter in a separate compartment, as it were. Modern science has radically changed this. Science has demolished the walls between the 'living' and the 'non-living'. We now place matter and life together, and mind separate from them. The 'impenetrable barrier' is between mind on the one hand and life and matter on the other.

Mental is not Examinable as a Form of Energy

Mind is not energy. It is not localizable in space and time. It is not easy to fully appreciate this situation. It is this which is the central theme of Charles Sherrington's book *Man on his Nature* (Cambridge University Press, 1951). Observes Sherrington, one of the greatest physiologists of all times; "The mental is not examinable as a form of energy. That in brief is the gap which parts psychiatry with physiology. Thoughts, feelings, and so on are not amenable to energy (matter) concept. They lie outside it. Therefore they lie outside Natural Science... In some ways this is embarrassing for biology. Biology as its name says is the study of life... Natural science has studied life to the extent of explaining away life as any radically separate category of phenomena... there is no radical scientific difference between living and dead... But though living is analysable and describable by natural science, that associate of living, thought, escapes and remains refractory to natural science... Our mental experience is not open to observation through any sense-organ ... Mind, for anything perception can compass, goes therefore in our spatial world more ghostly than a ghost. Invisible, intangible, it is a thing not even of outline, it is not a 'thing'. It remains without sensual confirmation, and remains without it for ever".

The mind includes the conscious as also the unconscious which perhaps is the very much 'larger' part. Any repetitive experience which has been fully learnt by us, and which is not likely to change, passes on into the unconscious. This may in course of time, if beneficial to the species, may be embedded through the process of evolutionary selection in the gene complex, the repository of inherited characters. At any moment of time all living individuals — men, animals, plants — present at that time constitute, as it were, the 'top' of the ever-growing 'tree' of organic evolution. The 'front' represented by the growing-points of evolution is continually moving onwards.

Each individual makes its contribution howsoever small — infinitesimally small — to the march of evolution.

In man his large brain with the characteristic frontal lobe is the dominant organ. It is the organ that has developed almost explosively in the last few million years. It has made man the master of the world. Ironically, this very situation has made man the most dangerous enemy of his own kind. He must learn to survive. He must learn to control himself, his passions, his material ambitions, and his utter selfishness, or else he will perish. Man will destroy man.

In man the brain (mind) represents the apex, the front, of the evolutionary process. In man the evolutionary process has for the first time in Nature become a conscious process. It can be directed by man. Unlike other species, man can exercise a measure of choice, an option, about his or her individual contribution to evolution, to man's future. This is a measure of man's dignity as also of his unique responsibility and obligation.

Evolution is Self-conquest

The mind, the centre of activity of the evolutionary process in man is the scene of confrontation, of clash, between man's 'animal nature' and his 'human nature'. The former is a dangerous relic of the past ages and it needs to be subordinated. The latter needs to be strengthened and reinforced. In brief, the process of man's onward evolution is a process of self-conquest. In the inimitable words of Erwin Schroedinger to whom we largely owe the idea so inadequately expressed above: "We are evolving. In every day of our lives there occurs in us something of that evolution of our species which is still in full career. In fact every individual life, indeed every day in the life of an individual, has to represent a part, however small, of this evolution, a chisel-stroke, however insignificant, on the eternally unfinished statue of our species. For the whole of its tremendous evolution consists of myriads of such insignificant chisel-strokes. And so at every step we have to change, overcome, destroy the form which we have had hitherto. The resistance of our primitive desires, which we encounter at every step, seems to me to have its physical correlate in the resistance of the existing form to the shaping chisel. For we are at once both chisel and block, overcoming and overcome — there is a real, continuous *self-conquest*."

And he continues: "... it is a *fact* that for every normally constituted human being now-a-days, unselfishness is the unquestioned *theoretical* standard of value, the ideal criterion of action — however infinitely remote his own actions may be from that criterion. In this very remarkable fact, almost inconceivable in its contrast with the actual behaviour of men, I perceive an indication that we are at the beginning of a biological transformation from egoistic to altruistic attitudes".

The quotation is from Schroedinger's essay, Seek for the Road, which he wrote at the age of 35 years, a few months before his epoch-making discovery of wave mechanics. [E. Schroedinger, *My View of the World*, Cambridge University Press (1964) pp. 54,58].

The concept of self-conquest leading to *action without attachment* constitute the central theme of Indian philosophy and ethics. It is expounded with unsurpassed insight and zest in the *Gita*: The Gita is *par excellence* the text for man's onward evolution.

Reference to Schroedinger encourages me at this point to draw attention to his ideas on the unity of all minds into *One Mind*. We have our individual minds, completely separate from one another, and yet we all discover that our experiences of the external world are similar — that is, it is the *same* external world we all observe. But, why should it be at all so? This leads to the metaphysical doctrine of *identity*, the unique discovery, as bold as it is profound, of the great thinkers of the *Upanishads*.

Science deals with the external objective world. It does not and cannot deal with the inner world of subjective experience. Its concern is matter and not mind. It cannot discover consciousness and mind (soul) because these are excluded by the very methodology and language of science. We do not find them in science because we have ourselves taken them out. The entire development and success of science has depended absolutely on this exclusion of consciousness, but perhaps the price paid for this exclusion has not been little. The present rather ominous disenchantment with science in some of the young may be related to it. It is not that the exclusion principle was imposed on science or deliberately formulated to guide its course. In the early phase of science the material and the non-material (rational and magical) were all mixed up together. (For instance, the *Gita* says that food grows out of rain, and rain out of *Yagna*: that digestion of food is a property of the soul. The latter is very similar to the Western view till about the eighteenth century).

The *exclusion principle* has emerged gradually with the growth of science. Now it reigns supreme. Perhaps, not quite exactly now.

We ask: What is the current status as science goes to the problem of mind-matter, the riddle of riddles? I shall attempt to answer very briefly from the standpoint of a physicist.

There are two different view-points.

Quantum Mechanics and Consciousness

The one holds that the question of mind-matter relationship is outside natural science because "the mental is not examinable as a form of energy." Science is *objective*.* It is quantitative and *deterministic*. (We are using the world "deterministic" *not* in the sense of the rigid determinism of classical mechanics, but in the sense of *causality*). The very possibility of physical science depends on well-defined equations of motion for physical systems, *e.g.* Schroedinger's equation in quantum mechanics.

* What we mean by objective is best described in the words of Karl R. Popper, the great logician of science [K.R. Popper, *The Logic of Scientific Discovery*, Hutchinson of London (1959) p. 44] "The words 'objective' and 'subjective' are philosophical terms heavily burdened with a heritage of contradictory usages and of inconclusive and interminable discussions. My use of the terms of 'objective' 'subjective' is not unlike Kant's. He uses the word 'objective' to indicate that scientific knowledge should be *justifiable*, independently of anybody's whim; a justification is 'objective' if in principle it can be tested and understood by anybody. If something is valid; he writes, 'for everybody in possession of his reason, then its grounds are objective and sufficient'."

Mind is subjective. It is not quantitative and not deterministic. We feel certain within us that we are free to think as we like (not necessarily free to express it). What guides mental activity is purpose — not an equation of motive. As mind by its very nature (consciousness or soul — the latter word is out of fashion these days) is outside science, the question of mind-matter interaction is not a valid scientific question. It is a pseudo-question. (One could say that by enlarging the scope of science one could include mind within it, but that would be saying that "Science" includes "non-Science".) There is psycho-physical parallelism between mind and brain, but a bridge between the psychical and the physical is in principle impossible. (It does not exclude direct interaction between one mind and another mind?) We may for brevity refer to this view-point as the Sherrington-Schroedinger principle. There is the other view-point which holds that mind-matter interaction is not outside science. The unravelling of the subtle mind-matter interaction may require, may even force upon us, a radical revision of the concept of space and time and matter and energy, but it is a problem within and not outside the domain of scientific investigation.

This view-point assumes that there is a 'bridge' between the psychical and the physical and this can, in principle, be investigated using the techniques and the conceptual framework of science. The merit of this view-point is that it is suggestive of investigation and exploration. Now that scientific techniques and instrumentation (and development in mathematics and statistics) have attained a level of accuracy, sensitivity and sophistication many orders of magnitude even beyond those available at the beginning of the century, it may well be worthwhile to direct fresh attention to the study of mind-matter interaction; of course, such studies to be of any value at all must need to be conducted with the utmost candour and highest standards of scientific integrity and objectivity. We may refer to this second view-point as the Neumann-Wigner principle.

John Von Neumann was the first, following the lead of Niels Bohr, to recognise clearly and discuss in detail that quantum mechanics forces us to admit two distinct kinds of processes which change the state of a physical (atomic) system. The one is described by the equations of motion and is valid so long as the system is left undisturbed. This excludes totally and completely any measurement or observation of the system. For, unlike classical mechanics, the very basis of quantum mechanics is that in the very nature of things it is impossible — impossible even in principle — to conceive of a measurement which will not disturb the state of the system. This minimum disturbance is such that it cannot be eliminated or analysed and allowed for. [It will not do to introduce 'hidden parameters' for the system and assume that it is ignorance about these which prevent analysis of the 'disturbance'. For a recent discussion of the problem see J.S. Bell, Rev. Mod. Phys. **38**, 447 (1966); E.P. Wigner, Amer. J. Phys. **38**, 1005 (1970)]. The concept of measurement in quantum mechanics is incomplete without reference to consciousness, as was shown by John Von Neumann. This is a point of great significance, though often overlooked in the usual expositions of Quantum Mechanics. The two types of changes occurring in the state of a system, one in the absence of measurement and the other accompanying measurement, belong to two totally different categories. The one is subject to the quantum equations of motion and the other is not. The latter process is also referred to as "reduction of the wave packet". Says Von Neumann: "The difference between these two processes is a very fundamental one. It is inherently entirely correct that the measurement or the related process of the subjective perception is a new entity relative to the physical environment and is not reducible to the latter. Indeed, subjective perception leads us into the intellectual inner life of the individual, which is extra-observational by its very nature (since it must be taken for granted by any conceivable observation or experiment)", [John Von Neumann, *Mathematical Foundations of Quantum Mechanics*, Princeton University Press (1955) Chapter VI].

We may conclude this discussion with the observation of E.P. Wigner: "We know far too little of the proportion and the working of the consciousness to propose a philosophy on a scientific basic. In particular, the "reduction of the wave packet" enters quantum mechanical theory as a *daus ex machine,* without any relation to the other laws of this theory. Nevertheless, the fact that the laws of inanimate nature, at least at one stage of the development, could not be formulated without reference to the consciousness remains significant."

And let us always remember what Karl Popper has said so eloquently: "The old scientific ideal of episteme — of absolutely certain, demonstrable knowledge — has proved to be an idol. The demand for scientific objectivity makes it inevitable that every scientific statement must remain tentative for ever. It may indeed be corroborated, but every corroboration is relative to other statements which, again, are tentative. Only in our subjective experiences of conviction, in our subjective faith, we can be 'absolutely certain'... The wrong view of science betrays itself in the craving to be right; for it is not his possession of knowledge, of irrefutable truth, that makes the man of science, but his persistent and recklessly critical quest for truth." [Karl R. Popper, *The Logic of Scientific Discovery*, Hutchinson of London) (1959), pp. 281-82].

Science and *Ahimsa*

In the West during the last three hundred years, the study of Nature has been pursued with unsurpassed vigour using the method of experiment and observation — an essentially new way of studying Nature which combined in a creative interaction mathematical concepts and measurement of things under controlled conditions. To put it crudely it was a joining together of crafts and philosophy. The resulting development of new technologies placed in the hands of western nations economic and military powers of an altogether new dimension. In the wake of the stypefying success these were pushed into the background, almost out of sight, such basic questions as what is the ultimate purpose of science? What is science for? On man's determination to pursue these fundamental questions in the age of the atom will depend not only the future of science but survival of society and civilisation itself. To transcend the age-old exploitation of man by man, to build a society reflecting both science and *ahimsa*, will need the combined effort and wisdom of both the Occident and the Orient.

A fundamental characteristic of our age is the close interaction, a coupling, between science, technology and productivity. Each reinforces the other, and this mutual reinforcement provides a rising spiral of science, technology and productivity — the S.T.P. — spiral, as it is called. But S.T.P. is not enough, not by any means. A long dark shadow of the S.T.P. spiral is the "armament race". In the context of our times, following World War II, releasing new aspirations and hopes of the common man, and with dominant emphasis on equality and egalitarian, the S.T.P. spiral is certain to, sooner or later, flounder and fail us, unless it embraces something much more than S.T.P. — unless a new dimension is added to it, the dimension of welfare and peace, in short of "wisdom".

The world may not blow up in the near future, but who can tell? Who can assure the hundreds of millions of men, women and children who want to lead peaceful, honest lives, that they and their children will not be reduced instantaneously to ashes at some unpredictable moment? The world is at a crucial stage. It is at cross-roads, facing a crisis like of which certainly has not happened in historical times. A solution has to be found and the basis can be nothing else than more and deeper knowledge, more science and more technology, directed to rational and beneficial ends. Once the world has become knowledge-based, as it is now, its future can only be on the basis of knowledge and never on its denial. Hiroshima and Vietnam are different, and so are Kalling and Jallanwala Bagh and yet in a fundamental sense there is something common that runs through them all. Violence is not divisible. We cannot eliminate it in one sector and applaud and retain in another. The S.T.P. spiral must be transformed into S.T.P. and peace (*ahimsa*).

15

Science and Vedanta*

Is Brahman the cause? Where are we born? Whereby do we live; and whither do we go? ... Should time, or nature, or necessity, or chance, or the elements be considered as the cause, or the who is called the pursha?

—*Svetasvatara Upanishad*

Erwin Schroedinger, a most distinguished physicist, and even greater as a natural philosopher, who received the Noble Prize for his epochal contribution to modern theoretical physics, writes: "A hundred years ago, perhaps, another man sat on this spot... Like you he was begotten of man and born of woman. He felt pain and brief joy as you do. *Was* he someone else? Was it not you yourself? What is this self of yours?... What clearly intelligible *scientific* meaning can this 'someone else' really have?... Looking and thinking in that manner you may suddenly come to see, in a flash, the profound rightness of the basic conviction in Vedanta... *This,* as we know, is what the Brahmins express in that sacred mystic formula which is yet really so simple and so clear; *Tat twam asi,* this is you. Or, again, in such words as "I am in the east and in the west, I am below and above. *I am this whole world.*"

And he continues: "It is the vision of this truth (of which the individual is seldom conscious in his actions) which underlies all morally valuable activity. It brings a man of nobility not only to risk his life for an end which he recognises or believes to be good, but — in rare cases — to lay it down in

---

*Bhavan's Journal *29,* (1) pp. 1-5, 1982.

full serenity, even when there is no prospect of saving his own person."

Schroedinger expressed these profoundly daring (certainly so in the western cultural milieu) and deeply moving thoughts in his essay, *Seek for the Road*. He wrote this a few months before his discovery of wave mechanics, a landmark in the history of twentieth century physics. The essay was first published with another, *What is Real?*, in 1961, under the title, *My View of the World*, thirty-five years after it was written. (The English translation of the German original was brought out by the Cambridge University Press in 1964).

Relevance of Indian Philosophic Thought

This reference to Schroedinger serves to emphasise the profound relevance, in the present age, of the Indian philosophic thought, and more recently of the great contribution of Sri Aurobindo. The Upanishads ask questions at the deepest level of our existence and with a daring and earnestness that is as inspiring as it is matchless and incomparable. Take for example the opening stanza of the Kena Upanishad: "By whom missioned falls the mind-shot to its mark? By whom yoked does the first life-breath move forward on its paths? By whom impelled is this word that men speak? What God set eye and ear to their workings?" It is therefore not surprising if we find a kind of creative resonance between the spirit of the Upanishads and that of modern science, particularly its most fundamental part, theoretical physics. The limitations of language, of words, in dealing with basic questions of existence (*e.g.* what am "I"?) was long recognised by the Upanishad thinkers. The recent development in physics have forced us to recognise the inherent limitation of language in describing atomic phenomena. P.A.M. Dirac, one of the most original physicist of our times and a Nobel Prize winner says: "The new theories, if one looks apart from their mathematical setting, are built up from physical concepts which cannot be explained in terms of things previously known to the student, which cannot even be explained adequately in words at all.

Like the fundamental concepts (*e.g.* proximity, identity) which every one must learn on his arrival into the world, the newer concepts of physics can be mastered only by long familiarity with their properties and uses". The radically new situation in physics, symbolised by Niels Bohr's *principle of complementarity* can help us, in a sense, to understand somewhat more easily the thoughts of the Upanishads, but we shall not puruse this subject here.

There is an upsurge in science and technology as never before. The extraordinarily rapid growth of science in the last three hundred years has proved immensely fruitful, successful, beyond all expectations. And yet, as never before, there is a sense of inner disquiet, a restlessness of the *soul*, that is deeply disturbing. It is increasingly affecting the youth, especially in countries most advanced in science and industrialisation.

Science is Universal

Science is *universal*. This is a fact of observation, and a most inspiring one. The laws of motion which describe the trajectory of a falling stone serve also to describe the motion of the moon, and other planets. This terrifically important discovery in science, and in man's intellectual history, was made by Newton barely three hundred years ago. To take another example of the universality of science, the atoms on our earth are identical with those in the sun and the stars, near and distant as revealed by observation and analysis of the light received from them. A central theme of science has been that every advance in science has re-inforced its universality.

Despite the very severe limitations of space and time to which man's body (which includes the brain) is subject to, man's mind is capable of "understanding" the physical universe. The realm of the mind is not circumscribed by the realm of the body. Not only that. The mathematical description of nature at the fundamental level has turned out to be astonishingly simple and beautiful. Indeed, a physical theory which is "mathematically beautiful" is likely to prove closer to nature, more successful and fruitful, than one which is mathematically ugly. Sir James Jeans exclaimed that God appears to be a pure mathematician.

Science is Objective

The most significant and basic characteristic of science is doubtlessly the objectivity of science. (Universality is a fruit of science, but objectivity is its seed, its foundation.) Science and objectivity are inseparable. We take it as axiomatic that a scientific "explanation" can contain no reference to, no intervention by, any supernatural agency, benevolent or malicious. In natural science there is no place for anything which does not satisfy the rigid criteria of logical reasoning. It is concerned with only "facts" that can be verified by experiment and observation. This demands that description of facts and theories in science should be unambiguously communicable from one person to another. Progress in science contributes to, and depends on, precision of "language". In this context "language" includes mathematics. Mathematics is necessarily precise and unambiguous. It is this which gives to mathematics a supreme place in science.

It is important to recognise that the objectivity of science, now taken as self-evident, has been achieved only gradually with the development of science over the centuries. When Newton explained the motion of the planet on the basis of his law of gravitation, he was unable to account for the stability (over a long period of time) of the solar system. He invoked, therefore, intervention by God to restore from time to time stability to the system (against the planets' mutual gravitational interactions). It was the French mathematician-astronomer Laplace who, nearly a hundred years later availing of the advances in mathematics, since Newton, proved that the solar system was stable. When Napoleon asked Laplace why there was no reference to God in his astronomical treatise, Laplace answered that he found no need for it. To Newton intervention by God to prevent disruption of the solar system was a point in favour of his gravitation theory. It revealed directly (scientifically?) the living presence of God. To take another example, again from Newton, to account for the indivisibility of atoms, he wrote in his great work on *Optiks* that no earthly power could set atoms asunder because God had made them indivisible. But an "explanation" (which involves the idea of purpose of any kind) is completely objective, not projective. This is its basic axiom. The greatest achievement of modern science, its most profound success, is the growth and strengthening of man's conviction, his faith in science, in reason.

It is the modern man's faith that what is not within the reach of reason today, will come within its reach some day, if man can continue his strivings, unfettered, undeterred and undaunted. There are no barriers that science may not one day penetrate. Science is autonomous. In a sense, the replacement of 'God' of Newton's *Principia* and *Optiks* by 'Faith in Reason' is the meaning of the autonomy of science. There is a certain similarity in the concept of the autonomy of science and the *Samkhya* concept expounded in the Upanishads. An illuminating exposition of the *Samkhya* is given by Sri Aurobindo in his Essays on the Gita (the Chapter on the Determinism on Nature).

The objectivity of science makes it truly and effectively, a co-operative enterprise which can be shared by all men. Dogmatism of any kind whatsoever is not admissible in science. Dogmatism is *subjective*. Its ultimate basis is *personal* belief, not reason or argument. Dogma is personal, science is public. Dogmatism and objectivity are a flagrant contradiction. The cooperative enterprise of science has been amazingly successful, far more than any other enterprise of man, but the objectivity of science is not without its price — and a very big price. It imposes a vital and most far-reaching limitation to which we now turn.

Exclusion of "I"

Science by excluding subjectivity cannot, even in principle, deal with our thoughts, feelings, emotions, with subjective experience of any kind. It excludes 'I'. The exclusion is total. Our feelings — pain, joy, or what not — are inherently incapable of unambiguous communication. Even if I succeed in expressing in words some particular feeling or emotional state of mind, there is no proof, there can be no proof, that these words will produce within you an identical "feeling". "I", consciousness, mind, or soul, or whatever name we may give to subjectivity (or to any aspect of it), has no place in science. We should note that what is excluded is the *mind* and not, of course, the *brain*. Brain can be investigated objectively; and recent developments in electronics have provided powerful techniques. The objectivity of science excludes *from it* "I": its *autonomy* excludes *from it* "God". Science is a deeply inspiring pursuit of objective truth; but its domain is by definition incomplete. Science is objective; but faith in science and in the pursuit of science demands a *subjective* decision. It is a *moral* quality. (In the *Samkhya* a distinction is made between atma (individual soul), and ahamkar, buddhi and mana, we use the word *mind* to include all these 'entities').

Brain and Mind: Mind is not a "Thing"

For a moment let us go back to the basic distinction between *brain* and *mind*. Brain is objective, mind subjective. When, for instance, sound waves impinge on our ears, the pressure changes of sound waves produce electric currents in the nerve fibres which from the ear reach the brain. How do these electric currents in the brain transform in the mind into sensations of sound. The same applies to other sensations. Science provides no answer to this riddle, the riddle of all riddles? The point to appreciate is that science by its very nature, its very objectivity, can give no answer. Science does not, and cannot, deal with sensation, and thought. To quote Sir Charles Sherrington, one of the greatest physiologists of our times (*Man on His Nature*, Cambridge University Press, 1951, pp. 228-57): "The mental is not examinable as a form of energy. That in brief is the gap which parts psychiatry with physiology... Thoughts, feelings, and so on are not amenable to energy (matter) concept. They lie outside it. Therefore they lie outside Natural Science ... In some ways this is embarrassing for biology. Biology as its name says is the study of life... Natural Science has studied life to the extent of explaining away life as any radically separate category of phenomena... there is no radical scientific difference between living and dead... But though living is analysable and describable by natural science, that associate of living, thought, escapes and remains refractory to natural science... Our mental experience is not open to observation through any sense-organ ... Mind, for anything perception can compass, goes therefore in or spatial world more ghostly than a ghost. Invisible, intangible, it is a thing not even of outline, it is not a "thing". It remains without sensual confirmation, and remains without it for ever."

Principle of Objectivation

At this point, if not earlier, the question is bound to arise that if mind is outside science, then, how does it create science. All experience, everything without exception, is fundamentally a personal experience: it is subjective. When you and I look at a tree, there is no conceivable way of determining that my sensation of "green" is the same as yours. That your perception and mine of a given thing is the same has no clear, no objective, meaning. How is objective knowledge then possible? This is not an easy thing to explain. The basic point is that an objective statement is not, and cannot be, about one single sense impression (say, my sensation of red colour produced by a flower), but it expresses always some relation between two sense impressions. My sense impression of red may be (or may not be — who knows?) different from yours, but it is a verifiable, objective statement that two given flowers are of the same colour or they are not. This simple example can be readily generalised. The essence of the matter is that objective, communicable statements become possible when we consider pairs of sense impressions — not about single sense impressions. This is called the *principle of objectivation*. It is this which is the basis of the objectivity of science. "The fact that by comparing pairs communicable, objective statements are possible, has an immense importance because it is the root of speaking and writing, and of the most powerful instrument of thinking, of mathematics." (Max Born, *My Life and My Views*, 1968, Chapter Five "Symbol and Reality").

Mathematical Logic

The conclusion that mind is outside the realm of objective science is extremely uneasy and tantalizing. How can anything, in principle, be outside science? What could be more "natural" than to assume that mind has evolved from matter, an accompaniment of the evolution of the brain, as a part of the long process of organic evolution. However, if the methodology of science is carefully analysed, there seems to be no escape from the Sherrington-Schroedinger conclusion that mind, by its very nature, cannot be described in objective scientific terms. Another consideration in support of this view is based on recent development in mathematical logic. It is of great interest, and is fundamental but subtle. Let me quote from the Noble Prize lecture (December 1969) by M. Delbruck (*Scientific World*, Vol.14, p. 15, 1970): "...our friends the (mathematical) logicians have made it clear to us long ago that in any but the simplest languages we must distinguish between an object language" and a 'metalanguage'. The word 'truth', and thus all discussion of truth, must be excluded from the object language if the language is to be kept free of antinomies. There then follows the strange result that there must be sentences that are true but not provable."

And he says: "Thus, even if we learn to speak about consciousness as an emergent property of nerve nets, even if we learn to understand the processes that lead to abstraction, reasoning, and language, still any such development presupposes a notion of truth that is prior to all these efforts and that cannot be conceived as an emergent property of it, an emergent property of a biological evolution. Our conviction of the truth of the sentence, "The number of prime numbers is infinite", *must be independent of nerve nets and of evolution*, if truth is to be a meaningful word at all" (italics added).

Separate Minds

If the mind is not a "thing", and if it cannot be described in terms of space and time, then the concept of *separate* minds — as many minds as there are bodies — has no clear meaning. The idea of separation implies localisation in space, and is therefore not applicable to mind: mind is not a "thing". This leads irresistibly to the grand Vedantic concept of ONE MIND. We shall return to this presently.

Mind-Body Interaction

If the mind is not a "thing", how can it interact with the body which is a "thing". If the mind cannot interact with the body, cannot influence its activity, how can an individual be held responsible for his acts, the actions of his body? If my mind (my thoughts) does not influence the movement of the pen in my hand, who is writing this sentence? On the other hand, if the mind does influence and determine the action of the body, how is such interaction possible? How can an entity not describable in terms of space and energy interact with matter and influence its motion. How do drugs — and there are plenty of them and available in increasing abundance — affect the state of the mind, if there be no interaction between matter (drugs) and mind? Do "I" have any influence, any control over my actions, or is everything my body does (all actions are performed by the body) determined precisely by the equations of motion which completely specify the motion of (all) material things? Is free-will a reality or is it an illusion? And if free-will has no reality, then moral responsibility, compassion, repentance and the like have little meaning. *All this totally defies understanding.* The phenomenal progress in science in our times has only served to deepen the mystery of the mind-body interaction. It has made the situation more disquieting than ever before.

We may recall two recent articles in the *New Scientist*. Professor D.M. MacKay (*New Scientist*, 2 July 1970) argues against determinism, whereas Professor John Taylor (*New Scientist*, 30 September 1971) reaches the opposite conclusion.

His thesis is that brain research is yielding increasing evidence in favour of determinism and against the concept of free-will. For him mind is only a "shadow".

We may also refer to the books, *The Interpretation of Nature and the Psyche*: C.G. Jung and W. Pauli, and Synchronicity, an acausal connecting principle. Jung says that the synchronicity principle advanced by him may help to "clear up the body-soul problem". He says: The "absolute knowledge" which is characteristic of synchronistic phenomena, a knowledge not mediated by the sense organs, supports the hypothesis of a self-subsistent meaning, or even expresses its existence. Such a form of existence can only be transcendental, science, as the knowledge of future or spatially distant events shows, it is contained in a psychically relative space and time, that is to say in an irrepresentable space-time continuum".

An interesting schematic representation of the physical-psychical situation which Jung presents, after discussion with Pauli, is shown in the figure below. Synchronicity deals with phenomena that are inexplicable not merely because the cause is unknown, but for them a "cause is not even thinkable in intellectual terms".

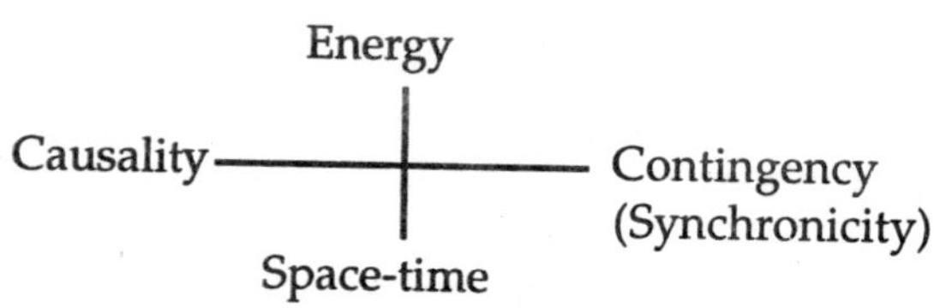

The mind-body paradox is as alive as ever. It is deeply disturbing and at the root of much of the restlessness and frustration affecting man's spirit today. It is in this sense that Sri Aurobindo is so relevant to the contemporary situation.

In the words of Erwin Schroedinger the only "solution" to the unfathomable mind-body paradox, "in so far as any is available to us at all, lies in the ancient wisdom of the Upanishads."

Self = SELF. The human body, like that of any other animal, is composed of atoms and molecules. The molecular organisation is extraordinarily complex and many of its features it would take a long time to unravel. Yet the basic "chemical units" are the same throughout the whole range of living organisms, animals and plants. These are twenty aminoacids and four types of nucleotides. This is a demonstration of an evolutionary process which, starting with simple atoms and molecules, has over some thousand billion years led to the present plant and animal kingdoms. In terms of complexity of organisation there is nothing (in the known universe) even remotely comparable to the human brain.

The recent far-reaching discoveries in molecular biology serve to provide beginnings of a framework for description, in physical terms, of the evolutionary process. The view is reinforced that the source of evolution is random fluctuation, over billion of years, operating at the molecular level. This operates in combination with the extraordinary fidelity (stability) of the mechanism of duplication of genes (macromolecules) responsible for transmission of hereditary characteristics from one generation to another. All this is explicable in terms of physics and chemistry. Jacques Monod has emphasised in his recent extremely fascinating and thought-provoking book [*Chance and Necessity — An Essay on the Natural Philosophy of Modern Biology* (1970), p. 110] that, "...chance alone is at the source of every innovation of all creation in the biosphere. Pure chance, absolutely pure but blind, at the very root of the stupendous edifice of evolution: this central concept of modern biology is no longer one among other possible or even conceivable hypotheses. It is today the sole conceivable hypothesis, the only one compatible with observed and tested facts. And nothing warrants the supposition (or the hope) that conceptions about this should, or even could, be revised". This is a grand affirmation of the objectivity and autonomy of science. A scientific study of biological evolution reveals, can reveal, no underlying purpose — no underlying design or goal towards which evolution is moving or directed. It could not be otherwise, as we have repeatedly emphasised. No considerations of purpose, divine or human, nothing which implies value judgements, can enter the gateway of objective science. The exclusive is total: Science by its very axioms is objective, not projective. If we ask: What purpose do the stars in the sky serve? The answer of astronomy is: The stars serve no purpose what ever. In the realm of objective science any other answer would be an absurd answer.

What we know about living organisms is not much, but we know enough to be able to conclude that the human body is a machine. It is so beyond question, subject to the laws of the physics and chemistry which make no distinction at all whether the atoms are parts of a living body or dead matter. Equally, one cannot deny the incontrovertible direct experience that the motions of his or her body are under his or her control. My body is a "machine", but "I" control its movements. Any other assumption would be unacceptable, unreasonable to most people. Let us assume as undisputed the two facts that (1) my body is a machine, and (2) its motions are under my control. From these two "facts" what is the inference we can draw which would not be contradictory to science—not violate its basic axiom of objectivity and autonomy? The only possible inference (as Schroedinger observes) is that every mind that has ever said or felt "I" is the person (if any) who controls the 'motions of the atoms', controls the universe, according to the Laws of Nature. This is the Vedanta formula: *self = SELF**

---

* Modern Physics, to which Schroedinger made such a crucial contribution, provides a helpful analogy. An electron, in fact, any physical entity on the atomic scale, shows both particle and wave properties. The two concepts, particle and wave, are sharply opposed to each other — one contradicts the other. The strange thing, totally unexpected, is that in the description of atomic phenomena both the concepts are essential: the two concepts provide complementary description. Nature is so made that an experimental arrangement designed to test the particle aspect automatically excludes an experimental arrangement to test the wave aspect. The two experimental conditions are mutually exclusive. Every act of observation is accompanied by a certain "disturbance" which cannot be eliminated and which is inherent in the nature of things. This is spoken of as the Heisenberg's principle of uncertainty. It is this uncertainty principle which accounts for the mutual exclusion of experimental arrangements for investigation of wave and particle properties.

An appreciation of the complementarity of the relation, self = SELF (the complementarity of the many and the ONE) cannot be achieved within the framework of objective knowledge. It needs its equivalent of the "principle of uncertainty."

The formula, self = SELF, is simple as a formula, but how to comprehend it and activate it in one's life. What is the way? Says Sri Aurobindo (in the concluding chapter of the *Essays on the Gita*): "Follow... the law of your Swadharma, do the action that is demanded by your Swabhava whatever it may be. Reject all motive of egoism, all initiation by self-will, all rule of desire, until you can make the complete surrender of all the ways of your being to the Supreme... A supreme Presence within you will take up your Yoga and carry it swiftly along the lines of your Swabhava to its consummate completion. And afterwards whatever your way of life and mode of action, you will be consciously living, acting and moving in him and the Divine Power will act through you in your every inner and outer motion. This is the supreme way because it is the highest secret and mystery and yet an inner movement progressively realisable by all. This is the deepest and most intimate truth of your real, your spiritual existence."

16

Science and Values*

The emblem of the Academy has on it the Sanskrit inscription (हयामि भर्गः सवितुर्वरेण्यम्) which says that a prime concern (dedication) of the Academy should be promotion and increment of human values. The message of the inscription has never been more relevant and needed than today. It brings to mind Einstein's deeply inspiring statement (November 1950):

"The most important human endeavour is the striving for morality in our action. Our inner balance and even our very existence depend on it. Only morality in our actions can give beauty and dignity to life.

"To make this a living force and bring it to clear consciousness is perhaps the foremost task of education.

"The foundation of morality should not be made dependent on myth nor tied to any authority lest doubt about the myth or about the legitimacy of the authority should imperil the foundation of sound judgement and action."

Mankind is today at crossroads. One path leads to despair and annihilation, the other to possibilities of boundless advancement and enrichment — material, cultural and moral-spiritual. Man has now reached a stage in evolution when his very survival and future evolution is possible only on the basis of Science and *Ahimsa*. *Ahimsa* is love and non-violence in word, thought and deed. And this gives a new role and significance to education — that is to the teacher — as never before in human history. Hopefully, there is convergence of new far-reaching developments in diverse fields of science

---

* Proceedings Golden Jubilee Celebrations, INSA, Delhi, pp. 123-33, – January 1984.

— from pure mathematics, and quantum mechanics and cosmology to molecular biology, socio-biology and psychology — pointing towards a more unified world view of knowledge and values.

Perhaps, the most basic and most revolutionary concepts are of the infinite in mathematics (leading to Goedel incompleteness theorem) and the principle of complementarity in physics. And the supreme value is *Ahimsa*. What is of the utmost significance for the future of man is that Science is providing new insights into it, opening up new possibilities and new tools for practice of *Ahimsa*.

Gandhi described *Ahimsa* as the farthest limit of humility. And he stated: "It was only when I had learnt to reduce myself to zero that I was able to evolve the power of Satyagraha". The foundation of *Ahimsa* and Satyagraha is self-control, self-discipline. In *Hind Swaraj*, Gandhiji said that real Swaraj is self-rule or self-control. That is the Gandhian path, its core.

In March 1951, Einstein declared: "Revolution without the use of violence was the method by which Gandhi brought liberation of India. It is my firm belief that the problem of bringing peace to the world on a supra national basis will be solved only by employing Gandhi's method on a large scale.

"Gandhi, the greatest political genius of our time, indicated the path to be taken. He gave proof of what sacrifice man is capable once he has discovered the right path. His work on behalf of India's liberation is living testimony to the fact that man's will, sustained by indomitable conviction, is more powerful than material forces and that seems insurmountable."

Any discussion of science and non-violence brings to mind the recent work of Konrad Lorenz and others which has shown that in Nature harmony is the normal rule and conflict an exception. Members of the same species never kill one another. Their fights are either sport or ritual. There are a few species which deviate from the rule. And the greatest exception is the human species. Homo Sapiens torture and murder one another in war and peace, with an abandon, wantonness and brutality that has no parallel in Nature. It is Man's gift to Nature. Within a span of 40 years, two World Wars killed many tens of millions of people. How deep and pervasive are the effects of GHD (Greed, Hatred and Delusion)? More than 60 per cent of all world's research and development work in science and technology is directed to military end; $600 million a year is the global military expenditure, and it is still increasing. Some 700 million human beings are living today in absolute poverty — hungry, illiterate, and disease-ridden. The link between the two is apparent. Total comprehensive disarmament and elimination of global poverty go together.

The food problem of poor countries has been aggravated by large increase in recent decades in consumption of animal protein by people in rich countries. A third of the world's yearly total output of cereals is used as animal feed to produce animal protein. About 5-20 kilos of vegetable protein go to produce a kilo of animal protein. This is done by industrial animal breeding methods of unspeakable cruelty. We cannot be cruel to animals and except that it will not harden human sensibility towards fellow human beings. In the long run, cruelty is indivisible, so is compassion. Alfred Kaestler (of optical pumping fame) at a UNESCO Conference in June 1978 observed that since animals are our "biological brothers", the time has come that in the interest of man's own future, "this relationship is legally recognised". The suffering of animals and of man is in the end not separable. No longer the rigid Aristotle Descartes partition between human beings and other living creatures is tenable scientifically. It is totally unreasonable and harmful.

In the advancement of the theory and practice of *Ahimsa*, science and technology can play a major role of which the education is perhaps the most significant. Science opens up for man possibilities of moral experiments and of insight into reality and ourselves as never before. It can help to liberate us from fear, greed, delusion and prejudice. And this continuing liberation opens up new horizons for exploration of nature and of Man's relations to nature. Every human action has a moral-spiritual component. And advancement of science can provide new opportunities and new tools for enlargement and enrichment of the scope and depth of our moral endeavour.

Science and technology can tell us what can be done and what cannot be done. Science describes the limits of the possible. But *science cannot tell us what we ought to do. That decision is an ethical-moral decision.* Scientific truths and moral truths are not contradictory. *These are complementary.* It is the exploration and practice of the complementarity of scientific and moral truths that gives to life richness and beauty and happiness. The principle of complementarity in modern physics provides an illuminating and clear illustration of the complementarity approach. It can serve to help the appreciation of the complementarity, outside and *beyond* physics of science and humanism (morality).

There is, as it were, a hierarchy or levels of complementarities, beginning with the wave-particle duality in physics and leading to many levels, and to the complementarity of body and mind of *prakrati* and *purusha* of the *Sankhya Darshan.* There is also the complementarity of the two hemispheres of the brain which is of central importance for man's behaviour (R.W. Spery, *Science*, 24, Sept. 1982). Bohr fervently hoped that the complementarity principle, in the near future will find a place in school education. It was his deep conviction that the approach suggested by the complementarity principle would serve as a most valuable guide in meeting life's problems, social and ethical. The complementarity approach is very similar to Jain and Buddhist logic. The chapter on Identity and Non-identity in gospel of Buddha by Paul Carus is most illuminating for an understanding of the complementarity approach.

Science properly taught, can contribute much and effectively to the incorporation of the moral component in education — central to man's progress and even survival in the Atomic Age. The task is by no means easy: it demands sustained, imaginative, and dedicated effort. The need is desperate. The Academy can make a significant and pioneering contribution. A basic element of education ought to be the theory and practice of how to subdue our *real enemies*: *Kama* and *Krodha* (greed, hatred, delusion). Nothing could be of greater value in life and for the welfare and progress of the community and mankind. How to make even a beginning in this direction needs intensive study and research.

To man's great good fortune, science-perhaps unexpectedly — is now slowly but steadfastly moving towards a more unified world view which includes *both* knowledge and values as complementary and mutually reinforcing.

17

S-T and Concern for the People*

The characteristic of the present century, unlike earlier times, is the close interaction — coupling — between Science, Technology and Productivity (S-T-P). This direct and intimate coupling between S, T and P is a new phenomenon. It gives rise to the exponential rate of growth of S-T. The doubling period of S-T is about ten years and in some areas of current science much less — for example, Computer Science and Technology. The fantastically rapid growth of science and technology arises from expansion of current areas of S and T and from discovery of new areas. Often these "new areas" are of totally unexpected, unforeseeable, content richness and potentiality. The so-called "doubling period of science" is the time it takes for doubling of the number of scientists, the number of research publications, the doubling of the R & D expenditure, and so on.

But S-T and P by themselves are not enough to ensure advancement of a nation and its well-being. Indeed at stake is the very survival of mankind in the Atomic Age. Perhaps no one realised this more sensitively and deeply than Jawaharlal Nehru. In stirring words Nehru said: "Science today gives us power to build up in this world a physical paradise for all. Science also threatens to consume this world, which would be hell-fire. What would you choose, this physical paradise or hell-fire? It is for the human mind and human spirit to be tempered by something and that something is spirituality, which gives us to some extent the right measure, the right perspective and right direction to look at."

---

*Proc. Indian Natn. Sci. Aca. *56A*, No. 2, pp. 137-144, 1990.

The progress of society depends ultimately on its willingness and capacity to seek truth and to regard pursuit of truth as its highest duty and obligation. Declared Nehru: "The true scientist is the sage unattached to life and the fruits of action, even seeking truth wheresoever this guest might lead him. To tie himself to a fixed anchorage, from which there is no moving, is to give up that search and to become static in a dynamic world." [*Science Reporter*, C.S.I.R. New Delhi (1964)]. The roots of scientific endeavour, as indeed of all truly creative effort, are essentially spiritual.

S-T-P by themselves cannot generate and ensure national development. For that we need with S-T-P a real passionate *concern for the people*, specially the poor and underprivileged.

Nehru was the General President at the 1947 Indian Science Congress held in Delhi. In moving words he said: "For a hungry man or hungry woman, Truth has little meaning. He wants food. And India is a hungry starving country, and to talk of Truth and God, and even of many of the fine things of life, to the millions who are starving is a mockery. We have to find food for them, clothing, housing, education, health and so on, all the absolute necessities of life that every man should possess."

And so *Science must think in terms of millions, and billions, of people*. More perhaps than any other man in history Nehru in his inimitable way and tireless energy communicated to the people the message of science — the limitations and the strength of science, its relentless and fearless quest of truth. He loved people and children and respected them, their intelligence and their sense of values and commitment.

The key issue in national development, the real problem and challenge, as Nehru always emphasised, is how to join S-T-P, integrate it, with passionate and effective concern for well being and advancement of all people, particularly in desperate need of even the barest necessities of life. It is an imperative obligation — material, moral and spiritual — to give the highest priority to this task. And it is by no means an easy task. It is overwhelmingly difficult to promote and achieve a real concern for the people — serious and sincere concern as distinct from pretensions. In this task the role and contribution of science and technology, and specially education, can be of the utmost significance and value. The object deserves to the utmost an earnest and sustained consideration by Educational Institutions and Academies. Every step counts.

In the world there was never so much S-T-P as today; and never before in man's history so much greed, hatred and brutal violence as today. There is a growing dehumanisation and decay of humanness. It is growing at a frighteningly rapid pace. There is almost a total disregard of human values and suffering of the poor and the destitute. Two World Wars in one century. Now "Drug" and "Aids". The total military expenditure in 1979-88 for the USA was $290 billion (6.0 per cent of the GNP). The USSR military expenditure is estimated at about $250 billion (SIPRI Yearbook, 1989). The world total of military expenditure may be taken as dollar 1,000 billion a year, that is, $250 per man, woman and child in the world. It is $2 million per minute. Notice that per man, woman and child the average yearly expenditure for *development and production of instruments of hate and cruelty and violence is $250.* It exceeds the per capita GNP in many Third World Countries. In agonizing contrast the expenditure on education and promotion of *Ahimsa* is almost nothing.

The tragic fact today is that globally nearly all S-T development is directed to means for men to kill one another, and too little, almost nothing, for men to love one another. The scientific community and the Academies have an undeniable obligation towards overcoming this deeply distressing situation.

The estimated number of test explosions between 6 July 1945 to 31 December 1988 is (SIPRI Yearbook 1989).

USA	*USSR*	*UK*	*France*	*China*	*India*	
910 (1945)	636 (1949)	41 (1952)	172 (1960)	31 (1964)	1 (1974)	Total: 1,790
Tests in 1988						
14	17	0	8	1	0	Total: 40

The brackets give the date of the first explosion. The total number of explosions before the signing of the Partial Test Ban Treaty (5 August 1963), prohibiting atmospheric tests, was 547 of which 425 were atmospheric tests. The lesson is unambiguous.

National development depends on a growth of the GNP. But this by itself does not lead to an improvement in the welfare and quality of life of the people, especially the poor. That demands above all the *concern for the people*. This is grossly, lamentably, inadequate and ineffective in all countries. It is inseparable from the tragic phenomenon of devastation and pollution of the environment. The most affluent countries are no exception. *It is a global phenomenon.*

How shall we grade, estimate, concern for the people? How shall we generate and promote it and strengthen it? The scientific community has a special role and obligation. It should receive our serious consideration. These are not easy things but profoundly important for development. A telling fact about a country's concern for the poors is the proportion of poor children in the total population. We may define, rather arbitrarily, a "poor family" as one whose per capita income is less than one-fifth the national average per capita. In the USA, the most affluent nation, 20 per cent of children live in families with incomes below the "poverty line". This is the most distressing situation (Mary Jo Bane and David T. Ellwood, *Science*, 8 September 1989). It would be far worse for most of the Third World Countries: studies need to be urgently organised, possibly with UNESCO support. These would be highly rewarding. Statistics are of great value and give a lot of information. But we must not forget that in human terms the suffering of one is no less significant and agonizing, as of the many. Percentage is quantitative, suffering is qualitative.

The basic *human value*, the foundation of all enduring progress and development, is *man's loving concern for the man, and indeed for all living beings*. It is "striving for morality in our actions." In this supremely important task, in the Atomic Age, science and science education has a crucial role and contribution to make of the utmost significance. Einstein in his unforgettale words (1950) on the foremost task of education says [INSA, *Albert Einstein* (1984), p. 24]:

"The most important human endeavour is the striving for morality in our actions. Our inner balance and even our very existence depend on it. Only morality in our actions can give beauty and dignity to life.

"To make this a driving force and bring it to clear consciousness is perhaps the foremost task of education.

"The foundation of morality should not be made dependent on myth nor tied to any authority lest doubt about the myth or about the legitimacy of the authority imperil the foundation of sound judgement and action."

True education for Mahatma Gandhi was *building of character*.

To sum up: The key to national development is science and technology, and building of character and concern for the people, particularly, the poor. Character building and true S-T-Development go together, mutually reinforcing.

In the Atomic Age national interests and of mankind are inseparable. Honest concern for the people should be the basic of all technology assessment. Almost every S-T advancement in the absence of *concern for the people* as is the case today, widens further the dismally large gap between the rich and poor countries and between the rich and poor *within* a country.

In a world dominated by science and technology promotion of effective *concern for the people, particularly the poor,* should be the foremost task of education at all levels. It should include knowledge of the aspirations, need and living conditions of the poor, productive work experience, and effective participation in community-social service. The meaning and practical importance as a guide in life and actions, of the *complimentarity principle* which is the foundation of the physics and philosophy of science of our century should be emphasised. It is *indispensible for the practice of Ahimsa*.

This conference provides exceptional opportunities for discussion and exchange of ideas. Apart from *concern for the people,* the basis of all development, some topics of dominant interest are:

1. Rising costs of S-T books and journals, far beyond the means of the Third World Countries.
2. Mathematics and Science Education in Schools.
3. Biotechnological Revolution.
4. Age of Computers and "Electronic Brain" — Critical importance of Brain-Mind Distinction.

These are directly related to the theme of S-T and Development. Take (1). Without availability of the indispensible S-T books and journals there can be little advance in the country of S-T research and education. [The yearly subscription of Nature is $195, of Science $320, of Physical Review $ 4,000 (nearly $6 per 100 pages), and of Physical Review Letter it is $800.] How many libraries in our country can afford the essential books and journals? The cost of the Russian publications is far less, about a tenth of the American and European publications. Here is an important lesson for us. There is also the need to promote a much more extensive use of the existing libraries. The entire subject merits detailed examination by the Academy.

A few words about school education would not be out of place. The standard and content of mathematics and science education requires a revolutionary reform. It is a global problem and challenge. It is an outstanding field for international collaboration. The writing of first rate books for schools is a first rate research effort. It needs a continuing programme involving active participation of eminent mathematicians and scientists, school teachers, and students. School education has to be integrated with the Biotechnological Revolution and Computer Revolution.

The imperative need for radical reform is universally recognised. But there is not much clarity about what to do and how to do it? Hard, sustained thinking is required, far more than is the case generally. The situation is unprecedented.

Today's world is *science and technology based* and, therefore, unpredictable in many essential respects. It is unpredictable because major scientific discoveries are by their very nature unpredictable. There has therefore to be a built-in flexibility in the entire educational system so that adjustments with rapid change are possible. These considerations underscore, for national development, the extreme importance of proper teacher education, of the commitment and creativity of teachers. These need every possible support and encouragement.

The Computer Revolution is likely to generate an educational and social transformation in some respects more profound than that brought about by the invention of the printing press five hundred years ago. In connection with the Biotechnological Revolution and the Computer Revolution may I refer to a question which, though generally ignored, in the past and even today, is likely in the coming years to acquire far-reaching significance for every aspect of our life and work. It is the question of all questions: It is at the root of all questions, scientific, philosophical and others. *It is at the root of all development — personal, national, international.*

The question is: Am I free, in some measure at least, to act as I please, and, therefore, answerable, and responsible for my actions? Or, is it that my body being an assembly of atoms and molecules and actions of my body are totally accountable in terms of space-time and matter-energy? Everything, all my actions are subject to determinism and chance. For an assembly of atoms and molecules, for a 'machine', there is no freedom, no choice, no creativity.

On the basis of available knowledge of S and T we prepare alternative development plans. We then make a choice between them for implementation. The question is: *Are we free to choose between alternatives*? Or, is freedom an illusion, and all course of development pre-determined by the laws of quantum mechanics governing the atoms and molecules constituting our bodies? Determinism for a material system (our body) is the undeniable, unambiguous lesson of modern science.

Notice that true, real freedom implies freedom to go against dictates of reason: to act unwisely if I so choose. We ought not to do this but we do this far more often than we realise. The freedom exercised by "I" by the *self* goes beyond reason. Nothing can shake our *faith* that in some measure at least "We" have real freedom. We act on that faith. Morality has no meaning without that faith. The fundamental question is Free Will and Determinism can no longer be evaded by the youth in a civilisation increasingly dominated by *Planck's Constant* and dramatic developments in biotechnology and computers. What is the source of free will? Where does it originate? We have to explore in all possible ways the *complementarity of brain (atom) and mind (self)*. [*NPL Bulletin*, New Delhi, Nov. 1989].

An illuminating example of the complementarity of freedom and determinism is provided by the following two statements of Einstein [INSA, Einstein (1984) pp. 24-25]. Free will or choice of action is inherent in Einstein's statement: "Caring for man and his destiny must always constitute the principal interest of all technical efforts. Never forget that in the midst of your diagrams and equations." Consider the other statement of Einstein which denies free will. "I do not at all believe in human freedom in the philosophical sense. Everybody acts not only under external compulsion but also in accordance with inner necessity. Schopenhaaer's saying, *"A man can do what he wants, but not want what he wants,"* has been very real inspiration to me since my youth; it has been a continued consolation in the face life's hardships, my own and others, and an unfailing well-spring of tolerance". A clue to perception of the complementarity of free will and determinism is provided when we recognise that both free will and determinism are rooted not in Reason, but in Beyond Reason. Free will and Determinism are two complementary aspects of the same Transcendenal Reality. Determinism is rooted in Beyond Reason, Beyond Science. The physical mathematical laws — and these are supremely, indescribably, beautiful — that account for space time and matter energy and atoms cannot originate within space time. To account for the very existence of space time, the laws cannot be within space time. The laws originate in the "self" and then manifest in space time. The "self" is beyond space time. The theme is discussed in Atom and Self [(INSA Proceedings, New Delhi 1979-80, and in *NPL Bulletin*, New Delhi, 1989); also Einstein on Scientific Truth, INSA (1984) p. 23].

In the end it is our belief or faith as to "Who are we?" that gives a meaning and purpose to all S-T and Development. This needs to be underscored and explicitly recognised. It,is particularly significant to note that in our century science provides strong support; albeit indirect, to overcome the Cartesian Partition between phusis and psyche, or brain and mind, without of course any violation to the objectivity and autonomy of natural science. This is a task of uncommon difficulty. Many names in this connection immediately come to mind: Planck, Einstein, Bohr, Heisenberg, Pauli, Schroedinger, Sherrington...

If *S-T Development* is to serve the real needs and interests of the people much bold, unorthodox and hard thinking is necessary. Above all it demands sustained determination and social commitment. *Unwise Development* can result in unacceptable damage to environment and cause harm in many ways. To undo the harmful effects of Unwise Development — much more frequent than one may think — can be prohibitively expensive economically and politically.

It is no easy thing to define "wise development" and no easy thing to implement it. We are reminded of the parallel case of education. Everyone knows that education today is in desperate need of radical reform, but there is little clarity or consensus as to what it should be and how to realise it. From a conference such as this we can learn much, and derive inspiration, about the theory and practice of *"Wise Development"*. There is much to learn from exchange of ideas and experience. There should be some continuing programmes for this purpose.

Mahatma Gandhi has given what he called a "Talisman". It is an unfailing guide to Wise Development in the Atomic Age. Recall the face of the poorest and the weakest man whom you may have seen and ask yourself if the step you contemplate is going to be of any use to him. Will he gain anything by it? Will it restore him to a control over his own life and destiny? In other words, will it lead to Swaraj for the hungry and spiritually starving millions? [Mahatma Gandhi, August 1947].

S-T Development has unlimited potential and power. It is an unprecedental instrument, a formidable instrument. If wisely used it opens the path to continual progress in knowledge, happiness and wisdom. But used unwisely it can lead only in the Atomic Age to universal suffering and total disaster. We fervently hope that our deliberations, formal and informal, would benefit us greatly in many ways, and also contribute in some measure towards mankind's goal of a world based on Science and *Ahimsa*. That would be a befitting homage to Jawaharlal Nehru.

18

National Science Exhibition for Children

WELCOME ADDRESS
(14th November, 1971)

We feel greatly honoured and happy by the presence of our respected Rashtrapatiji, Shri V.V. Giri, at this inaugural function of the National Science Exhibition. We are deeply grateful to him. It is a great encouragement to all of us that he has so generously agreed to inaugurate the Exhibition.

The suggestion for the Science Exhibition came from the Jawaharlal Nehru Memorial Fund. We are greatly indebted to our Prime Minister, Shrimati Indira Gandhi, for her generous encouragement and support. We are grateful to Dr. Karan Singh who has taken a very keen interest and helped us always. The Jawaharlal Nehru Memorial Fund has made a major contribution towards the expenses of the Exhibition.

The task of organising the Exhibition has been entrusted to the National Council for Science Education (NCSE) working in close cooperation with the Council for Scientific and Industrial Research (CSIR), the National Council for Educational Research and Training (NCERT), and the UGC.

It is a great pleasure — ladies and gentlemen, participants, young friends and scientists of tomorrow — to welcome you to the Exhibition. I sincerely thank you. We are grateful to the many institutions and organisations — universities, I.I.T's, colleges and schools, NCERT, CSIR, National Laboratories, Atomic Energy Department, Meteorology Department, Defence Science Organisation and the Indian Agricultural Research Institute — for their cooperation and participation in the

Exhibition. The NCSE has received valuable support for the Exhibition from the NSF, the USAID, the West German Academic Exchange Service, the British Council, and the Ford Foundation. Our sincere thanks are due to them.

On this occasion our first thoughts turn naturally to Jawaharlal Nehru. Promotion of science and scientific humanism was a dominant passion of his life. His love for children and concern for their development and welfare was unabounded. It is most befitting that the National Science Exhibition with its emphasis on science education and science in the service of the community is inaugurated on the birthday of Nehru. And it is most propitious that the inauguration is by our esteemed Rashtrapatiji.

The purpose of the Science Exhibition is to promote science education and dissemination of science. A visit to the Exhibition gives us a "feel" of the excitement and creativity of science and technology. It helps to appreciate the great power and complexity of science, as also the deeply inspiring grandeur and beauty of scientific abstractions. Many examples of "mathematical beauty" immediately come to mind. A classic case is the discovery, based on the work of Professor S.N. Bose, that all particles in nature can be classified in terms of the symmetry of their wave functions: Particles are either *bosons* (named after BOSE) or *fermions* (named after FERMI).

An exhibition provides an occasion for cooperative effort and an opportunity to learn from one another's experience, students and teachers together. It reinforces initiative, innovation and creativity. A major aim of this Exhibition is to encourage a wide use for science education of easily available materials and local resources. The immense potentialities of adapting simple inexpensive things, toys and kits (strings and sealing-wax, to use an old phrase) for class experiments, demonstrations and teaching aids is not enough realised. We could learn far more by fully exploiting simple devices, from improvisations, than we would from expensive apparatus poorly used as is often the situation. In the first case one has got to think and do continuing research, whereas in the latter case it is largely a question of spending money — usually someone else's money.

The modern world is knowledge based, largely science and technology based. Two crucial questions for us and for nearly all countries (including the most advanced in science) are: *Firstly,* how can science and mathematics education (imparted on a large-scale) be made, for pupil and teacher, an exciting experience, relevant, creative, and humanistic. The response to this challenge has initiated a revolution in science and mathematics education. The *Second* question is: How science, growing at a terrific rate, can be 'popularised'. How can science and even more importantly the spirit of science, be communicated to the people without gross distortion and misrepresentation.

Science exhibitions, if carefully planned and organised, can make a significant contribution to these two themes. As regards popularisation of science, so essential for the health and progress of the nation, the difficulty is not that science is inherently difficult to communicate. In fact basically, science is easy to communicate. The real trouble is that specialists seldom make an earnest effort to make science accessible to non-specialists and to the common man. Many a specialist may lack the temperament for science popularisation but there is also a lack of opportunities and incentives. Science exhibitions provide opportunities for public communication of science. Let me mention that the standard definition of mathematics and science, of objective knowledge, is as Kant said, "If something is valid for anybody in possession of his reason, then its grounds are objective and sufficient." The test of science and mathematics is that, in principle, it should be communicable and comprehensible to any person in the street provided he is sane and is willing to give time. (Please understand all the implications of saying I cannot understand science.) To take into account current research on child-learning, we could say that 'any person' should also include young children. It is now becoming increasingly apparent that the capabilities of young children to grasp abstract mathematical and scientific concepts have been in the past very much, if not grossly, underrated. This brings us to the revolution, still in its early stage, in science and mathematics education. It started some 20 years ago. It began with a few scientifically advanced countries, notably the USSR and the USA. The events of the World War II and the post-war years have emphasised the extreme importance of science for national development and welfare, and the wide public interest generated by atomic energy, big computers (and automation in industry), and the satellites. The need for a radical change in science education has been felt everywhere for a long time, but it is only recently that significant activity has begun.

The way science is taught today to most pupils in most countries, it hardly helps to promote curiosity and the spirit of inquiry. In fact, not unoften, it tends to kill questioning, creativity and originality: Science as generally taught kills the spirit of science. We recall the words of Albert Einstein: He says about his life at the Polytechnic Institute of Zurich which he entered at the age of 17:

"The mass of insufficiently connected experimental data was overwhelming here also. In this field, however, I soon learned to scent out that which was able to lead to fundamentals and to turn aside from everything else, from the multitude of things which clutter up the mind and divert it from the essential. The hitch in this was, of course, the fact of that one had to cram all this stuff into one's mind for the examinations, whether one liked it or not. This coercion had such a deterring effect (upon me) that, after I had passed the final examination, I found the consideration of any scientific problems distasteful to me for an entire year. In justice I must add, moreover, that in Switzerland we had to suffer far less under such coercion, which smothers every truly scientific impulse, than is the case in many another locality. There were altogether only two examinations; aside from these, one could just about do as one pleased. This was especially the case if one had a friend, as did I, who attended the lectures regularly and who worked over their content conscientiously. This gave one freedom in the choice of pursuits until a few months before the examination, a freedom which I enjoyed to a great extent and have gladly taken into the bargain the bad conscience connected with it as by far the lesser evil. It is, in fact, nothing short of a miracle that the modern methods of instruction have not yet entirely strangled the holy curiosity of inquiry; for this delicate little plant, aside from stimulation, stands mainly in need of freedom; without this it goes to wreck and ruin without fail. It is a very grave mistake to think that the enjoyment of seeing and searching can be promoted by means of coercion and sense of duty". (Albert Einstein: *The Library of Living Philosophers*, 1949, p. 17).

In the last 10 years in several countries much effort has been devoted towards a radical reform of course-contents, and teaching of school-science and mathematics. UNESCO has evinced great interest in, and encouraged, these activities. The OECD had made an important contribution. The process of science-education reform is a long and difficult one. It demands perseverance, dedication and resources. A significant development is an increasing collaboration between school teachers, university teachers and research scientists. This is a relatively new thing, and it is crucially important for science education. It deserves every possible encouragement and support. We have been rather fortunate in this respect. This Exhibition at the NPL campus, and to which the NPL, under the inspiring leadership of its Director, has contributed so much (at an unbelievably short notice) is in itself a splendid example of the collaboration between schools, universities and research laboratories. A part of Exhibition — the NCERT exhibits and from schools — is located at the Bal Bhavan on the Kotla Road.

To Dr. Verma and his colleagues, and to Kumari Shanta Gandhi and staff of the Bal Bhavan, we are grateful for the time and attention they have given to the Exhibition. There are many persons from Delhi and outside whom I should mention for their generous help and participation, but claiming on their indulgence I shall thank them without referring to their names. Dr. R.D. Deshpande and his colleagues, and Shri Rajan, have (as usual) worked with remarkable zeal and dedication. We cannot thank them adequately. We are grateful to Shri S.N. Johar for providing accommodation at the Sri Aurobindo Ashram to a large number of participants.

The number of exhibits put up by students from different parts of the country is about 2,000. These have been selected by an expert committee. The response from students and teachers has been most enthusiastic and encouraging, beyond expectations. There would have been very many more exhibits but for severe limitations of space and even more the limitations of funds.

The National Science Exhibition programme for improvement of science education and dissemination of science has to be a continuing and expanding one, part of the national movement — not confined to big cities but extending to towns and villages. To learn science is to do science; and one can do a lot of interesting science, especially biological science, with readily available materials and appliances in homes and farms. Also, every college and school can make a significant contribution to popularisation of science. To build up an effective programme of science exhibitions on a large scale would need considerable planning and preparatory work; cooperation of schools, colleges and research institutions; hard work and ruthless economy in expenditure — each one helping others to cut down costs, and not the other way round.

Besides general exhibitions, it is also proposed to organize special exhibitions, dealing with subjects such as computer science, microbiology, materials science, earth sciences, and so on. The NCSE in cooperation with the CSIR, INSA and the Indian Science Congress Association could make an important contribution to the development of the National Science Exhibition programme.

Bibliography

Ackerman, Peter and Duvall, Jack: *A Force More Powerful*, Palgrave, New York 2004.

Ahmed F. editor: *Atom and Self*, Collection of Lectures Delivered by D.S. Kothari New Age International Publishers, New Delhi, 2002.

Ahmed, F. editor: *Science and Humanism*, Collection of Articles, Addresses and speeches Delivered by D.S. Kothari, Golgotia Publishers, New Delhi, 2004.

Aurobindo, Sri: *The Upnishads*, Pondicherry, 1972.

Capta, Fritjof : *The Tao of Physics*, Fontana, England, 1980.

Carus, Paul: *Gospel of Buddha*, National Book Trust, New Delhi, 1981.

Dossey, Larry: *Meaning and Medicine*, Bantam Books, 1991.

Fulghum, Robert: *All I really Need to know I Learned in Kindergarten*, Joy Books, New York, 1988.

Gandhi, M.K.: *An Autobiography, or The story of My Experiments with Truth*, Navjivan Publishing House, Ahmedabad, 2000.

Gandhi, M.K.: *Fellowship of Faiths and Unity of Religions*, Gandhi Book House, New Delhi, 1990.

Gandhi, M.K.: *Thought for the Day*, Publication Division, Ministry of Information and Broadcasting, Government of India, New Delhi 2000.

Gangrade, K.D.: *Gandhi's Autobiography: Moral Lessons*, Gandhi Smriti and Darshan Samiti, New Delhi, 1998.

Ganguli, B.N.: *Gandhi's Social Philosophy, Perspective and Relevance*, National Gandhi Museum, New Delhi, 2000.

Heisenberg, W.: *Physics and Beyond*, Harper and Row, London, 1971.

Hussain, Abid S.: *Gandhiji and Communal Unity*, Orient Longman, New Delhi, 1969.

Joshi, Kireet: *Philosophy of Value-Oriented Education: Theory and Practice*, Indian Council of Philosophical Research, New Delhi, 2002.

Kasner, E. and Newman, J: *Mathematics and the Imagination*, G. Bell and Sons, London, 1961.

Kothari, D.S.: *Nuclear Explosions and their Effects*, The Publication, Division, New Delhi, 1958.

Kothari, D.S.: *Some Thoughts on Science and Religion*, Sri Raj Krishan Jain Charitable Trust, New Delhi, 1977.

Parcham Lal and Dasta Lok [eds]: *Globalization of Capital, An Outline of Decent Changes in the Modus Operandi of Imperialism*: A Study

Commissioned by Lal Pancham and Lok Dasta, published by Rajwant Pal Singh and Subhash Gatade, Ahmedabad, 1997.

Popper, Karl: *Objective Knowledge, An Evolutionary Approach*, Clarendon Press, Oxford, 1972.

Ranade, R.D.: *Spiritual Awakening in Gandhi and other Indian Saints*, Sarva Seva Sangh Prakashan, Varanasi, 2003.

Rangnathananda, Swami: *Science and Religion*, Advaita Ashram, Kolkata, 1976.

Schrodinger, E.: *My View of the World*, Cambridge University Press, 1964.

Schrodinger, E.: *What is Life*? Cambridge University Press, 1948.

Sharp, Gene: *Gandhi as Political Stragetist, with Essays on Ethics and Politics*, Gandhi Media Centre, New Delhi [Indian Edition], 1999.

Sherrington, C.S.: *Man on His Nature*, Cambridge University Press,1940.

Srinivas M.N.: *Religion and Society among the Coorgs of South India*, Oxford University Press, New Delhi, 2003.

Stiglitz, Joseph: *The Roaring Nineties: Seeds of Destruction*, Allen Lane [an imprint of] Penguin Books, England, 2003.

Varma, Ravindra: *The Spiritual Basis of Satyagraha*, Navajivan Publishing House, Ahmedabad, 2001.

Gangrade K.D.: A Few Chapters in Edited Books

Continuum Social Work, in Social Work, Today, edited by Visversaran P.K. Madras School of Social Work, Golden Jubilee Commemorative Volume, 1999, pp. 173-75.

Environmental Crisis : A Challenge to Modern Civilization for Secularization of Environmental Stewardship, in *Social Environment for Sustainable Development*, editors, Joshi Y. G. and Verma D.K., Rawat Publications, Jaipur and New Delhi,1998, pp. 51-86.

Gandhi and Empowerment of Women— Miles to Go, in *Empowerment of Women Miles to Go* [ed] Singh Savita, Inter-national Centre of Gandhian Studies & Research, Gandhi Smriti and Darshan Samiti, 2001, pp. 42 73.

Who Rules the World? In *Public Governance and Decentralization*, [eds] Mishra S.N., Mishra Anil D. and Sweta Mishra, Mittal Publications, New Delhi, 2003, pp. 553-62.

Social Work—Changing Ideology of Relief, in *Social Action through Law—Partnership for Social Justice* [ed] Gandhi P.K., Concept Publishing Company, New Delhi, 1985, pp. 19-32.

Social Networks and Crisis Management in Indian Families: A Personal Account, in *Social Structure and Change*, Vol.5, Religion and Kinship [eds] Shah, A.M., Baviskar, B.S. and Ramaswamy, Sage Publications, New Delhi, 1998, pp. 111-34.

Human Development and Social Transformation—A Case Study, in, *Pursuit of Institutional Excellence* {Essays in Honour of V.K.N. Menon, [eds] Reddy Sanjeev P.L., Singh, Jaideep and Tiwari, P.K., *Indian Institute of Public Administration*, New Delhi, 2004, pp. 69-81.

Employee Morale: An Attitudinal Study of Workers, in, *The Concept of Work in Indian Society*, [ed] Moddie, A.D., Indian Institute of Advanced Study Shimla in association with Manohar publications, New Delhi, 1990, pp. 53-70.

Chavan, Sheshrao, *Gandhi and Ambedkar - Saviours of Untouchables*, Bhartiya Vidya Vhawan, Authors Press, Delhi, 2001.

Jain, R.B. and Bongartz, Heniz, *Structural Adjustment Public Policy and Bureaucracy in Developing Societies*, Har-Anand Publications, 1993.

Radhakrishnan N., *Gandhi: The Quest For Tolerance and Survival*, Gandhi Smriti and Darshan Samiti and Gandhi Media Centre, New Delhi, 1995

Humanising Development - The Gandhian Way, in *Gandhism after Gandhi* [ed] Mishra Anil Dutta, Mittal Publications New Delhi, 1999, pp 111-22.

Bhoodan and Gramdan: Revolution Through Love, in, *Gandhi in the Global Village*, [eds] Radhakrishnan, N. and Vasudevan, N., Gandhi Media Centre, New Delhi, Centre for Global Non-violence, Hawaii, 1998, pp. 274-88.

Environmental Crisis: A Challenge to Modern Civilization for Secularization of Environmental stewardship [ed], in Jain, R.B. *Environmental Stewardship and Sustainable Development*, Friedrich Ebert Stiftung, New Delhi, 1997, pp. 85-106.

Gandhi Through Five Generations - A Personal Account of Rural Social Work, in, *Social Work Practice*, [ed] Patel Chaya, Rawat Publications, Jaipur & Delhi, pp. 217-57.

Gandhian Perspective on Education, in, *Education for a Global Society* [ed] Mukhopadhyay, Shipra, New Delhi, 2003, pp. 40-52.

"Wake Up Calls" for India's Environmental Security or Face Collective suicide, in *Environmental Security*, [ed] Jain, R.B. Published by the International Institute for Environmental Strategies and Security, Canada, pp. 157-70.

Efficacy of Law as an instrument of Social Change - A case of Untouchability, in, *Social Exclusion* [ed] A.K. Lal, Concept Publishing Company, New Delhi, 2003, pp. 195-212.

Sardar Patel: Constitution Maker, in *Sardar Vallabhbhai Patel, The Nation Builder* [eds] Reddy Sanjeev, P.L. and Mishra, S.N., Indian Institute of Public Administration, New Delhi, 2004, pp. 212-23.

Critical Role of NGOs [Non-Governmental Organizations] in *Contemporary India*, [ed] Sinha, B.P. point of view, Published by Shri Ranchor Prasad Commemopation Committee, Patna, 2000, pp. 430-50.

Gandhi and Religion

Kher, V.B. [ed], *In Search of Supreme Gandhi, Mohandas Karamachand*, Navjivan Publishing House, Ahmedabad, 1961.

Chatterjee, Margaret, *Gandhi's Religious Thoughts*, Macmillan Press, London, 1983.

Anand J. Hingorani, *None High: None Low*, Gandhi, M.K., Bharatiya Vidya Bhawan, Bombay, 1965.

Rao, K.L. Seshagiri, *Mahatma Gandhi and Comparative Religion*, Motilal Banarasidass Pub., Delhi, 1978.

Hingorani, Anand, *Food for the Soul*, Bharatiya Vidya Bhawan, Bombay, 1970.

Hingorani, Anand T.(Ed.). *Law of Love*, Gandhi, M.K., Bhartiya Vidya Bhawan, Bombay, 1970.

Hingorani, Anand, *Why Fear or Mourn Death*, Gandhi, M.K., Bharatiya Vidya Bhawan, Bombay, 1971.

Mahatma Gandhi, *Contribution to Hinduism, Karna*, Classical Publication Co., New Delhi, 1981.

Gandhi, M.K., *Hindu Dharma*, Orient Paperback, New Delhi, 1978.

Kher, V.B., *The Essence of Hinduism*, Gandhi, M.K., Navjivan Publication House, Ahmedabad, 1987.

Betai, Ramesh S., *Gita and Gandhiji*, Gujarat Vidya Pith, Ahmedabad, 1970.

Desai, Mahadev, *The Gospel of Selfless Action or the Gita according to Gandhi*, Navajivan Pub. House, 1970.

Gandhi, M.K., *The Bhagvadgita*, Orient Paperback, New Delhi, 1991.

Discourses on the Gita, Gandhi, M.K., Translated by Desai, Chander V.G., Navjivan Publishing House, Ahmedabad, 1960.

Jag Parvesh ed., *Gita, the Mother*, Gandhi, M.K., Indian Printing Works, New Delhi, 1957.

Gandhi, M.K., *The message of the Gita*, Navajivan, Ahmedabad, 1959.

Teaching of the Gita, Gandhi, M.K. Ed., Hingorani, Anand T., Bharatiya Vidya Bhawan, Bombay, 1971.

Acknowledgements

Thanks are due to my grandson Vaibhav Gangrade, Mrs. Seema Sharma, Mr. Ramesh and Mrs. Shashwati Jhalani

Index